The Benedictine Abbey Of Ss. Mary, Peter, And Paul, At Pershore, Worcestershire... - Primary Source Edition

Francis Baugh Andrews

THE BENEDICTINE
ABBEY OF SS. MARY,
PETER, AND PAUL, AT
PERSHORE
BY FRANCIS B. ANDREWS,
A.R.I.B.A., ARCHITECT

Pershore Abbey, Worcestershire.

Pershore Abbey from the East.

The Benedictine Abbey
of SS. Mary, Peter, and Paul,
at Pershore, Worcestershire.

BY

FRANCIS B. ANDREWS, A.R.I.B.A.,

ARCHITECT.

BIRMINGHAM : Midland Educational Co. Ltd.
PERSHORE : Fearnside & Martin.
MDCCCCI.

Pershore Abbey, Worcestershire.

AUTHOR'S NOTE.

𝒙

In the preparation of this History every care has been taken to trace each point back to the most authentic source available, to which in many instances reference is made by footnotes, &c. ; and the effort throughout has been to secure reliability to the furthest detail in every record, either by pen or by pencil.

The Author's cordial thanks are due to the Vicar of Pershore, the Rev. J. H. Bridgwater, M.A., and to his predecessors, the Rev. J. A. Bell, M.A., and the Ven. Archdeacon Walters, M.A., for the continuing permit and facility that has been accorded to him in the preparation of the drawings, &c. Also to the Rev. T. A. Wolfendale, M.A., and the Rev. J. H. How, M.A., of Durham University, for translation and revision of the sentences of the *Charta Edgari* as given among the Addenda.

The Author is also much indebted to J. W. Willis-Bund, Esq., M.A., F.S.A., etc. ; Walter de Gray Birch, Esq., LL.D., F.S.A. ; and W. Salt Brassington, Esq., F.S.A., for their valuable suggestions in the course of the work.

F.B.A.

BIRMINGHAM,

April, 1901.

𝒙

Pershore Abbey *

Scale of Feet

north elevation

measured & drawn by Francis S. Andrews 1891

The Benedictine Abbey of
SS. Mary, Peter and Paul of Pershore,[1]
Worcestershire.

✗ ✗

PART I.—OF THE HISTORY.

"PEARESHORE showeth the ruynes of an Abbey builded in King Ædgar's raigne by Egelward, Duke of Dorsett, and hath a markett. And for the Abbie, although it is nowe, as the rest, nothing, yet I think longe before the suppression it was very much diminished with the increase of Westminster's Monasterie."

This Thomas Habington[2] wrote in the notes of his Survey of Worcestershire, and a statement more blind and erroneous could scarcely have been made, for only in the concluding words of it is there any truth at all, and the rest is absolutely wrong ; the fact is that the Abbey "Pershore shows" had not only an altogether earlier foundation and quite another man as its founder, but far from being "nothing" is of remarkable interest and beauty in each and all of its unique features, fragment though it be of its original extent. It has been well said otherwhere—"the Church is of peculiar interest, as well historically as from its intrinsic beauty . . . . . an invaluable relic of a glorious edifice."[3]

Pershore was one of the earlier, if not the earliest foundation in Worcestershire,[4] and in common with most other monastic institutions had to undergo many difficult and trying experiences, which recurred again and again, particularly during the turbulent times of its earlier years.

---

1 Pershore, from the Anglo-Saxon *pursh* = a willow, and *score* = shore ; not as some have supposed from the abundance of pear trees.
2 1560–1647.
3 Extract from a Report by the late Sir Gilbert Scott, R.A., 1862.
4 The date of Worcester being 680 (?), Evesham 701, Malvern 1083, Bordesley 1120 A.D. (?)

The frequency with which the buildings were damaged by fire, the ravages of successive invaders, and the rapacity of those with whom might and right were synonymous terms, have so far obscured the early history of the Monastery and its affairs as to make a continuous account of its existence practically impossible. Fragments, only, of its story are to be found here and there, and these often but occasional references in the writings of historians of other places, and such records were not always careful and cannot be entirely relied upon.

Of the original foundation, dates varying from as early as 604 A.D. to so late as 970 A.D. have been given in different records, but without much difficulty these may be sifted down to two, which seem to have an almost equal claim for rectitude. They are these—681 A.D., preferred by Dr. King[1] and Rev. Mackenzie E. Walcott,[2] and 689 A.D., given by Leland[3] and others, and generally accepted.

The confusion of opinion concerning the date and founder arises from various sources, but chiefly in the frequent restoration or refounding of the Monastery after devastation by fire or pillage, and also in the changes that occurred from time to time in its dedication, or in its alternate occupancy by secular clergy and monks; at such times the loss or destruction of its registers would leave no other authoritative record to be accepted than the earliest in those which replaced them, and in such, by error or by purpose, preceding events became obscured more and more completely with each succeeding change.

In 792 A.D. Egelward of Dorset completed or enlarged it[4]; and in the time of Coenulph, King of Mercia, a certain Duke named Beornoth (mentioned in Edgar's Charter) refounded it.

Its original founder is almost unanimously agreed upon by the various chroniclers; it was Oswald, the nephew of Ethelred I., King of Mercia; he, following the example of his brother Osric, who had founded Gloucester in 681 A.D., instituted at Pershore a house for secular or missionary clergy, and as he was so largely assisted in his efforts by the magnanimity of his royal uncle, doubt probably thus arose as to whether the King was not actually the founder himself.

Of one of the injuries received by the Monastery it is recorded that,[5] in the year 976 A.D., it was seized by a Mercian Duke, Ælfhere or Delfere, (a descendant, it has been said, of the founder), and was very considerably injured by him; this miscreant had made himself notorious at other places also by like deeds, and he is spoken of in a legend as having received at his death God's judgment on these sins in being eaten up by vermin. His son Oddo, earnestly deprecating the wickedness of his father, took a vow of celibacy lest any son of his should ever be guilty of such heinousness, and, not content with this, he and others set themselves to the work of repairing and rebuilding the injured Monastery, and, dying in 1056 A.D., he was buried in the Lady Chapel.

The lead coffin containing his remains was dug up in 1259 A.D., when excavations were being made for the pavement completing the Early English Lady Chapel[6]. The lid bore the following inscription :—" Odda Dux quondam, priscis temporibus Ædwinus vocatus in

---

1 King's " Munimenta Antiqua.'
2 Archæl. Assos. Journ., 1876 ; in a subsequent statement he gives 689 A.D., Engl. Minsts., vol. ii.
3 "In this year, 680, Abbess Hilda died. In these days the Monasteries of Pershore and Gloucester were founded by two brothers. . . . Pershore by Oswald . . . it was about the year 689 . . . when they were founded."—Leland Collectanea. vol. i.
4 W. Malmesbury.
5 "A.D. DCCCCLXXVJ. Quidam consul nequissimus Ælferus nomine. Persorevsem ecclesiam et plures per Angliam ecclesias miserabiliter destruxit. quas rex Eadgarus et Adelivoldus reverentissimus construxerunt.'—Cole MSS.
6 The bones of Abbot Foldbrith were also found at this time in another lead coffin near Oddo's.—Leland Coll. vol i.

baptismo, cultor Dei qui monachus effectus fuit ante mortem suam, hic requiescit. Sit ei gaudium in pace cum Christo Deo. Amen."

Florence of Worcester records thus of him :—A.D. 1056. "Earl Ethelwin—that is, Odda (Earl of Devon), the friend of churches, the solace of the poor, the protector of widows and orphans, the enemy of oppression, the shield of virginity- died at Deerhurst on the second of the calends of Sept. (Aug. 31st), having been made a monk by Aldred Bishop of Worcester before his death ; but he lies in the Abbey of Pershore, where he was buried with great pomp."[1]

The Anglo-Saxon Chronicle also mentions him in connection with Pershore :—"In this year (1056) died Earl Odda,[2] and his body lies at Pershore ; and he was ordained monk before his end, a good man and pure and very noble; and he died on the IInd of the Kal. of September."

The existing work of the south transept is said to be attributable to the efforts of this man ; it is the earliest now remaining.[3]

The Abbey of Pershore was at one time very wealthy, and its possessions extended to places at some distance. King Edgar's Charter,[4] in 972 A.D., mentioned and ratified one given at an earlier date, which had been obtained at the instance of Duke Beornoth ; it confirmed the estates, which consisted of upwards of three hundred and thirty-five manors or farms and other properties. But these possessions were subsequently much reduced, for to enrich the monks of Westminster, some of the Kings, and particularly Edward the Confessor and William the Conqueror, made over portions of the estates of various provincial Monasteries, and in this way Pershore suffered very considerably.

William of Malmesbury said it was miserable to observe how great damage this and other religious houses had sustained, having lost more than half their revenues, "Partem divitum occupavit ambitio, partem sepelivit oblivio, majusculam portionem reges Eduardus et Willelmus contulere Westmonasterio."[5]

Habington also says that : "Westminister's Monasterie hathe allso not onely a greate share in this hundred, but allso a part of Peareshore's towne ; for the Kings of England advanced Westminster, the Church of their coronations and sepulchers."

About the year 1086 A.D., on the compilation of the Domesday Book,[6] the Surveyors of King William recorded the estates of the Church of St. Mary of Pershore ; they appeared therein to amount to about one hundred and ten hides,[7] and also to include certain woods, salt refineries, etc., and some properties not mentioned in the earlier Charter ; they were located in Civintune (*Chivington ?*), Abberton. Wadborough, Broughton-Hacket, Edbretintune (*Abberton ?*), Wick, Comberton, Beoley, Stourbridge, Broadway, Leigh, Brandsford, and Mathon (*in Herefordshire*), and Cowley and Hawkesbury (*both in Gloucestershire*).

In this Survey also, Westminster was stated as holding considerable parts of Pershore, Droitwich, Pensham, Birlingham, Bricklehampton, Defford, Eckington, Besford, Longdon,

1 Chron. of Worc.; Hoveden also speaks in equal terms of him—i. 103.
2 Earl of Devon, &c., part of the possession of Godwin and his family. The Manor or Deerhurst, Leland says, Oddo gave to Pershore, and it was subsequently given by Edward the Confessor to Westminster.
3 E. A. Freeman considered this so, and gave 1056 as the date of the work.
4 vide Addendum I.
5 Chron. lib. iv.
6 For a reduced *fac-simile* of the portion relating hereto, with a translation, vide Addendum II.
7 There are some counter claims on some of the lands of doubtful right.

Powick, Upton, Snodsbury, Martin-Hussingtree, Dormston, North Piddle, Naunton, Beauchamp, Grafton, Flyford, Pirton, Wyre Piddle, Peopleton, Great and Little Comberton, Broughton-Hackett, Nafford, Severnstoke, etc., and four salt furnaces at Droitwich, the bulk of which properties belonged originally to Pershore.

Circset (church contribution on the first fruits of harvest) appears to have been paid on three hundred hides, though Pershore's actual possession was apparently only one-third of that extent.

x

The Monastery was at first instituted for secular or preaching clergy, the headquarters for their mission work in the district ; it was afterwards taken from them, either during actual occupancy or in their absence after some fire, and given to the monks, and from time to time was alternately held by one or the other.[1] It came eventually into the hands of the Benedictines (or Black Monks) through the influence and contrivance of Archbishop Dunstan, who, having appealed to King Edgar, about 960-965 A.D., for the appointment of Oswald to the then vacant bishopric of Worcester, and having gained that request, consecrated and enthroned him there himself. Whereupon Oswald, after having introduced the Benedictines into the Cathedral, in 969 A.D., extended his efforts to the various monasteries in his district, and at Westbury, Winchcombe, and Pershore, he ousted all the seculars who refused to take the monastic vows and habit of the order.[2] At the death of Edgar, however, another and temporarily successful effort was made to restore the secular clergy, but it was ultimately abandoned, and after a few years of disquietude the monks settled down, and in 983-4 A.D. Foldbrith is recorded[3] as the first Benedictine Abbot.

x

The fires that so frequently damaged the early structures of the Monastery were due in a large measure to the almost exclusive use of timber in the construction of the buildings of those days,[4] and although as the centuries advanced it was gradually superseded by stone, still the monks were often recorded as having to rebuild and repair their premises after disaster by fire. The first definite record of such is of the re-entry of the monks into a new church after a fire in 1020 A.D.[5]

In 1102 A.D. re-entry after another fire is recorded ; in rebuilding after which, as Gloucester was then practically complete, and the work at Tewkesbury well in hand, it may very possibly have been that the same school of masons who executed the Norman work at those places came on here also, and thus account be made for the similarity between the buildings in so many points.

In 1223 A.D.,[6] on St. Alban's or St. Urban's Day, the eastern arm of the church was entirely destroyed by fire, and the Abbot and his monks rebuilt it with the present magnificent structure. In this effort royal mandate was given for timber (some 36 trees) from the Crown forests ; and in 1239 the new work was consecrated by Cantelupe, Bishop of Worcester.[7]

---

1 Tanner, in Not. Mon., says : first seculars, then regulars, again seculars (or nuns, on Leland's authority), and from 984 Benedictines.—p 616
2 Leland : Coll., vol. i., says that the Benedictines first obtained the Monastery on its restoration after the depredations of Ælfhere ; but more probably Ælfhere ejected them shortly after Oswald had instituted them, and Leland is referring to their re-entry.
3 Ann. Wig.
4 Wood was used even in Domesday times, wherein is a reference to such in Yorkshire : "ibi presbyter et ecclesia lignea."
5 "Introitas fuit Persorensis novæ ecclesiæ post combustionem, et terræ motus subsecutus est."—Leland.
6 Ann. Wig. "Abbatia de Persorâ cum maximâ parte villæ, xiii. cal. Junii. conflagtavit."
7 Ann. Worc.

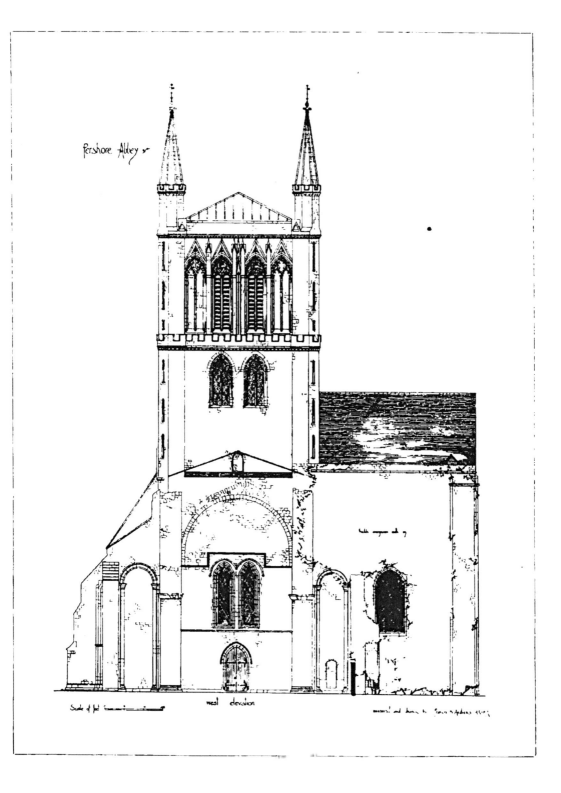

Pershore Abbey sr

Scale of feet

meal elevation

measured and drawn by Edwin A Andrews 1907

Another and most disastrous fire broke out in 1288 A.D. It occurred on the 22nd of April, originating in the bakehouse, whence it rapidly spread to the adjacent apartments, the bell tower,[1] and the Church, and was not abated until great destruction had been wrought, and some forty houses in the town had been burned down.[2] The domestic buildings of the Monastery were almost entirely destroyed, the Church was very much damaged, the Norman superstructure of the tower had fallen, and the nave, choir, and transepts were no doubt roofless and more or less injured by falling débris from the tower.[3] It was after this fire that the present vaulting of the choir and south transept was executed, and the lantern tower constructed on the arches of the crossing that remained standing, though doubtless needing considerable attention and repair.

✗

In aid of the Monastery, to assist in its rebuilding after fires, and for its general benefaction, gifts or grants were made at various times by the Crown.

At the time of its foundation Ethelred, King of Mercia, who was lavish in his gifts to those who were endeavouring to institute religious houses in his kingdom, gave much to Pershore, but between his time and that of the Confessor only Offa and Eadgar appear to have assisted it; this, however, is probably due to the loss of the records, for there can be no doubt that others were among its benefactors. Again, after another gap, John is next mentioned, and he, on Aug. 15th, 1204, visited Pershore, and sent a command to the sheriff of Gloucester to forward to the monks some casks of wine for one of the Feasts. Henry III. granted, in 1227 A.D., in aid after the fire of 1223, timber from the royal forests for its reconstruction, and also a fair to be held on St. Edburga's Feast and the two following days in the churchyard of Holy Cross, and by rentals of the ground for booths a considerable annual increase was made to the treasuries of the Monastery. Since 1836 the fair has been moved into the town, and is held in June. The holding of it in the churchyard caused much damage to the buildings and tombs which were misused on such occasions. Henry[4] granted also another fair to be held at Broadway, and yet another at Hawkesbury, and free warren rights in various royal preserves. Edward I. visited the town and stayed there eight days in 1281, and again in 1294. Edwards II. and III. also were benefactors of the Monastery, and Henrys V. and VI. granted the continuance of its former privileges, and in some small measure augmented them.

Other benefactions than those from royal hands were received by the Monastery. Of such it is recorded[5] that the sum of two shillings, to be paid yearly, was received by Abbot Leye about 1290 A.D. for lights in the Chapel of St. Mary; that one John, son of Thomas de Pershore, an inhabitant of the town, gave, about the same time, some land for the use of the Monastery and "for the good of his soul"; also to the Chapel of St. Michael the sum of £4 15s. 0d. and other land. Nash records that a certain Christopher Westerdale bequeathed 18d. for an annual mass to be said in the Chapel of St. John the Baptist. The principal benefactor in later times was Sir Adam de Hervington, or Hewington,[6] who gave one hundred and forty-three marks

1 Some melted fragments of bell metal were dug up at the time of the 1862 restorations.
2 Florence. Ann. Wigorn. "viii' cal. Maii ignis veniens de incendio pistrini et bracini Persorensis clocherium primo invasit et totam feré cremavit ecclesiam et de villâ plusquam xl. mansiones."
3 At the Restoration, 1862, considerable traces probably of this fire were found in the south transept walls, and insomuch was the stone damaged as to necessitate extensive repair.
4 11 and 35 Hen. III.   5 Deeds in Augm. Office; and other MSS.
6 Henry VIII. Survey of Chantries.

(£95 6s. 8d.), and land and houses valued at £10 per annum, to endow a chantry, and another sum of "nine marks of silver yearly" to the special priests of that chantry; the pension of the priest of this chapel was valued at £6 in Henry VIII.'s *Valor*, and the plate and ornaments are referred to as being valued at 4s. and 44s. respectively. Besides these[1] there are recorded some minor benefactions from various donors.

In 1277 and 1282 Pershore was required to assist in the wars with the Welsh,[2] and in 1346 Edward III. called upon it to subscribe one hundred marks for his French campaigns, and again in the following year it was required to send thither sacks of wool.

Richard II. entered into a bond for twenty marks with the Abbot of Pershore, who had granted him a loan for that amount.[3]

The dedication of the Abbey varied at different times in its history. In the Domesday it is called the Abbey of "*St. Mary*"; in Henry VIII's *Valor* of "*St. Edburga.*" It has also been called the Church of "*SS Mary Ædburga and Holy Cross*"[4] (the parochial portion was dedicated to the *Holy Cross*). In its earlier years *SS. Mary, Peter, and Paul*[5] were its patron saints, but at the time of the introduction of the Benedictines it was probably dedicated to *St. Mary*, with whom was joined *St. Ædburga*, whose relics had then not long been added to its treasures.[6] This latter saint is said to have been the third daughter of Edward the Elder, and grand-daughter of Alfred the Great; legend says that from infancy she evidenced inclinations towards religion, which on one occasion were tested by her father, who offered her a choice between jewels and toys and a book of the Gospels. She extended her hand not for the toys, but for the book, at which action the King was highly gratified, and took it to be a presage of the choice of life she would afterwards make. She became a nun, entered a convent at Winchester, and died there in 960 A.D. Some time afterwards Egilwado, nephew of the Abbess of that convent, obtained by special favour, and on payment of £100, some of her bones—the back portion of the skull, some ribs, and smaller bones—and brought them to Pershore, where they were placed in a gilt coffin; and tradition says that many miracles of healing were effected at the shrine wherein they lay.

Among other notes of the Abbey there are records that :—In 1259 A.D. the Lady Chapel was still in progress, probably nearly complete; ten years later a record speaks of great damage to the conventual buildings by wind; in 1327 the Monastery was said[7] to be in a very bad state both financially and structurally, unrepaired damages of fire—the nave in ruins, and the refectory, dormitory, hostelry, etc., in a dangerous state.

In 1345 A.D. permit was granted by Bishop Wolstan for the founding of a Chantry Chapel to Sir Adam de Hewington on the south side of the conventual church, and it was probably that at the east end of the south choir aisle or the one breaking out of it towards the south.

---

1 Habington also gives the following as benefactors, and states that their arms were blazoned on the windows :—Attwood, Beauchamp, Boteler, Clare, Le Despenser, Russell, and Vampage.
2 Palgrave Parl. Writs.   3 Shirley MSS.
4 In the Valor of Pope Nicholas (1288—1291) the altar of the Holy Cross is mentioned as being in the Church of the Monastery at Pershore. "Altare S. Crucis in Ecclesia conventuali de Persorâ sed parochiale."—Cott. MS.
5 Habington.
6 Obtained by Egilwado (or Ethelward Wada), and given by him to Pershore (Leland Coll.) He was said to have been one of Oddo's assistants in the restoration after the damage of Ælfhere.
7 Prattiton MS.

Concerning two of the Abbots the following incidents are recorded. The first is legendary, though it is given by the historian Ædmer as being entirely true. He tells of Abbot Foldbrith, that after death, as the body lay awaiting burial, it suddenly became rëanimated, arose, and sat erect. Some monks who were keeping vigil by it, with Abbot Germanus of Winchcombe, fled, but he, undismayed, demanded of the spirit in the name of the Lord that if the miracle was of heaven its cause should at once be made known. He replied that in heaven his sins had been charged against him by S. Benedict, but, through the fervency of the prayers of Oswald, he had been pardoned, and his mission was now to acquaint the world that Oswald was one of the greatest saints that had ever lived. Germanus asked how S. Benedict appeared in heaven, and how he was clad, to which the spirit replied that the holy saint "appeared most beautiful, and the most nobly clad of any, shining with precious stones, and attended by innumerable multitudes of monks and nuns, all most beautiful." After remaining half a day, the spirit finally departed.[1]

The other incident concerns Abbot Newnton. In 1427 A.D., one John Lockyer was accused of defaming the Abbot, and as a punishment was condemned to be whipped three times round Worcester market on market day, and as many times round Pershore Parish Church on Sunday, having only his shirt and breeches on, and to carry a taper of 6lbs. weight in his hand, which he was to offer after the reading of the Gospel, and to request the offended Abbot to scourge him as a penitent.[2]

At the suppression of religious houses in the 16th century we find further notice of Pershore.

To Thomas Cromwell--the Crown-appointed Vicar-General, who headed the Visitation Inquiry in 1535 A.D.—was addressed the following remarkable letter,[3] by Richard Beerley, one of the monks : —

"Most reverent Lord in God second person yn thys rem of Englond ynduyd with all grace and goodnes y submytt myselfe unto yoᵣ grace desiryng youᵘ to be good and gracyus lord vnto me synful and poor creatur. My lowly and myck scrybulling vnto yoᵣ nobull grace at thys tyme ys gruggyng yu my conchons that the relygyon wych we do obser and keype ys no rull of Sentt Benett nor yt no commandyment of God nor of no Sentt but lyzth and foulysse serymonys mayd sume yn old time and sume yn oᵣ tyme by lyzth and ondyscryttt faders wych have done ther dutys and fulfellyd ther owne serymonys an lett the preceps and commandyments of God go and so have y do thys syx yere wyche doth now greve my conchons sore that y have bye a dyssymblar so long tyme the wyche relygyon says Sentt Jamys ys yn vayne and brynggng forth no good frutts bettᵣ owtt then yn the relygyon except yt were the tru relygyon of Chryst also we do nothyng serch for the doctryn of Chryst but all fololoye oᵣ owne sensyaly and pleser and thys relygyon as y supposse ys all yn vayne glorry and nothyng worthy to be except nathur before God nor man. Also most gracyus lord ther ys a secrett thyng yn my conchons wyche do the move me to goo owt of the relygyon and yf yt were never so perfet wyche no man may know but my gostly fader the wych y suppos yf a man mothe juge yn other yong persons as yn me selfe for Chryst say nolite judicare et non judicabimini therefore y wyl juge my nowne conchons fyrst the wych fault he shall know of me heyr aftᵣ more largyorly and many other fowll vycys don a monckst

1 Malmesbury and others.   2 Noake.   3 Cott. MS.

relygyus men not relygyus men as y thynk the owtt not to be cald but dyssymblars wᵗ God. Now most gracyus lord and most worthyst vycytar that ever cam a moncks us helpe me owt of thys vayne relygyon and macke me yoʳ servant handemayd and beydman and save my sowlle wych shold be lost yf ye helpe yᵗ not the wych you may save wᵗ on word speckyng and mayk me wych am now nawtt to cum unto grace and goodnes. Now y wyll yustrux yoʳ grace sumwatt of relygyus men and how the kyngs graces commandyment ys keyp yn puttyng forth of bocks the beyschatt of roms vserpt power moncks drynk an bowl aftʳ collacyon tell ten or xii of the clock and cum to mattens as dronck as myss and sume at cards sume at dryss and at tabulls sume cum to mattens begēy sume at the myds and sume when yt ys all most done and wold not cum ther so only for boddly punnysment noᵗ thyng for Gods sayck wᵗ many other vycys the vse wych y have no leser now to express also abbotts moncks prests don lyttyl or nothyng to putt owt of bocks the beyschatt of romes name for y my selfe do know dyur's bocks wher ys name and hys vserpt powor apon vs ys. No more vnto yoʳ nobul grace at thys tyme but Jesu preserve you to pleser Amen. Your commyssary commandyd me to wrytt my mynd vnto yoʳ nobul grace by my outhe y toyk of hym yu oʳ chaptʳ hows.

To my nobull and gracyus lord	Be me yoʳ bedyman Dan
Vycytar yn the kyngs cortt be	Ryc Beeley now monck yn
thys byl delyvord yn hast.	the Monastery of Pershor."

This man was doubtless an imposter who had probably been placed at Pershore that his evidence might form the basis of the Commissioners' demands for the resignation of the Monastery. It was an expedient resorted to elsewhere, and the reports thus sent in were entered into a book called "The Black Book," which was laid on the table in the House of Commons in 1536 A.D.

On August 20th, 1534, John Poletensio, *Abbot ;* John Fladbury, *Prior ;* Thomas Persthore, *Third Prior ;* Robert Cheltene, *Sub-Prior ;* Richard Langley, *Firmarer ;* John Bradney, *Sacrist ;* James Brereton, Richard Mathon, *Chanter ;* Gilbert Burton, *Kitchener ;* Thos. Pepuetor ; John Compton, *Almoner ;* William Hawkesbury, *Succentor ;* Will. Worcester, *Sub-Sacrist ;* John Candycroft ; Richard Alcester, *Sacellar ;* John Ledbury, *Keeper of the Chapel ;* Thos. Upton, Andrew Streynsham, George Evysham, Thomas Walcott, and Richard Beerley, signed their names to the documents of the King's supremacy, and thus terminated the existence of the Monastery of Pershore.[1]

Henry settled pensions[2] on most of the Abbots and many of the Monks of the suppressed Monasteries ; at Pershore the Abbot received a pension of £160, in receipt of which he lived for some twenty years ; and the Monks received annuities in various sums to a total amount of £104.

In the book of Pensions in the Augmentation Office is as follows :—

      " Pshoʳ nup̄ Monastr̄rum in Com. Wigorn. surs'redd et dissolut'.

Pencōns assignyd unto the late abbott and monks yʳ by Robt Sowthwell Esquyer and others the kyngs hyeghnes comyssions appoyntyd to take surrender of the religious house in the countye of Worcetʳ to be payd unto the seyd abbot and monks yʳ duryng ther naturall

---

1 Pratt. MS., vol. xxvii.   2 Grant in Augm. Off.

lyffs at the feast of thanunciacon of o^r blessyd Lady the Virgyn and Seynt Michaell tharchangell yerely by equall porcons the fyrst payment to begyn at the feast of thanunciacon of o^r Lady next ensuyng thys day viz. the xxjth day of January in the xxxjth yere of o^r sovaign Kyng Henry the viiijth viz. to

John Stonewell busshop of Poleten' abbot y^r clx^{li.} of the gallarye new lodgyngs adjoynyng to the same on' garden ij. orchards, wth the pools in the same.

John Sondyford, prior	. .	xiij^{li.} vj^{s.} viij^{d.}
John Hyll, supprior .	. .	x^{li.}
Jamys Welys, kechynor	. .	vj^{li.} xiij^{s.} iiij^{d.}
Richard Pollen, almen'	. .	ix^{li.}
Gilbt Gybbyns, fermerar	. .	viij^{li.}
Willm Hybbold, sexten	. .	vj^{li.} xiij^{s.} iiij^{d.}
Thomas Hawkyns, celerar .	. .	vj^{li.} xiij^{s.} iiij^{d.}
John Survyor . .	. .	vj^{li.} xiij^s iiij^d
John Flyn . .	. .	vij^{li.}
Thomas Bradley .	. .	vj^{li.}
Willm Creyse . .	. .	vj^{li.}
Andrewe Dudley .	. .	vj^{li.}
George Phyllyps .	. .	vj^{li.}
Thomas Hethe . .	. .	vj^{li.}

Summa   cclxiiij^{li.}

Rob^r Sowthwell.
R. Gwent.
John Scudamore.
Rob't Burgoyn.
Thomas Acton."

And twenty years after a document shows that James Welys (called therein Jacob Wyllowys), Richard Pollen (Pulleyn), Gilbert Gybbyns (Gibbons), William Hybbold, John Survyor (Surveyour), John Glyn (Glynne), William Creyse (Cryes), George Phyllyps (Philippes), and Thomas Hethe (Heathe) were still in receipt of their pensions ; and some twenty-two others are also stated to be in receipt of annuities.[1]

The Abbey was valued, after it had passed into the hands of the Commissioners, at about £645. Dugdale gives it at £643 4s. 5d. ; Stevens at £633 13s. 11d. ; and Speed at £666 13s.

Sufficient money was not forthcoming to pay so large an amount, and therefore, of the fabric of the Church only the Choir, Transepts, and Tower, and their various Chapels were retained ; the Nave and Conventual buildings were demolished, and the materials variously disposed of.[2] It is difficult to assign a reason for the selection of the conventual portion of

1 1 and 3. Philip and Mary.
2 Used as building material in many subsequent erections in the town in which moulded stonework, carvings, &c., are frequently found on their demolition or may still be seen existing in them.

the Church (which is the part that was retained) in preference to the Nave that contained the parochial altar of the Holy Cross. In most cases where choice was compulsory the Nave was preferred, though at Milton, Little Malvern, Boxgrove, and a few other places, the choir, as here, was preferred.

The Abbey was granted[1] with the lands, buildings, vineyards, and manors of Old and New Pershore, Abbotswood, and Wadborough, and the fair and market of the town, with all the rights, privileges, liberties, and other valuables connected therewith, to William and Francis Sheldon. The grant cost £483 5s. 3d.

One of the MSS. of the Monastery—the *Chartulary* is now in the Augmentation Office. It consists of one hundred and sixteen vellum leaves, and contains various deeds, etc., none of which can be referred back earlier than the 13th Cent.; it was discovered in 1620 A.D., and then sent to the keeper of the Records of that Office.[2]

In the British Museum there are MSS. relating to Pershore from the 12th Cent., one of which contains the depositions of the Prior and others after a fire (*see addenda*); there is also a certificate concerning the Charter of Edgar. The Throckmorton MSS. include a commission from Pope Martin V. to the Abbot of Pershore permitting the alienation of Throckmorton Manor; also, among the MSS. at Little Malvern, are the land Charters of Henry VI. and Edward III. and another deed; and in the Birmingham Reference Library are three MSS. from the Sheldon Coll. Madox, in his *Formulare Anglicanum*, Nos. cliv., cxcviii., ccxxxvii., ccccxl., ccccxlix., and ccclix.; and Dugdale, in the *Monasticon Anglicanum*, vol. ii., 1846 edit., gives the text of various other MSS., etc.

Leland mentioned three MSS. that were in the Monastery Library in his time—" Ælfrici Grammatica Latino-Saxonica," " Parabolas Solomonis et Apocalypsim," by Bede, and " Extracts from Priscian."

Arms of Pershore Abbey

The present Registers date back to 1540 (32 Hen. VIII.),[3] but there is nothing of special note contained in them.

The arms of the Abbey at one time were : *sa,* a cross ragulée *or;*[4] at another, *sa,* on a chevron *or* between three ant-hills of the same, three holly leaves *proper* slipped (sometimes given as *vert,* and at others *azure*), on each hill four ants *proper.*[5]

There are several seals known now as belonging to the Abbey or its Abbots, though in the long course of its existence there were doubtless several more.

i.[1] A fine seal of the 12th Cent., pointed oval, about 3⅜in. long by 2¹³⁄₁₆in. broad. The inscription is—

✠ SIGILL · BEATE · MARIE · ET · SC̄E · EADBURGE VIRGINIS · PSORENSIS · ECLESIE.

It exhibits the Virgin with crown seated on a carved throne, on the left knee the Child with nimbus, lifting up His right hand in benediction, in her right hand a sceptre fleur-de-lizé. At the left side of her head a crescent, on the right an estoile of six points. On the left S. Paul standing, holding a sword erect by the point; on the right S. Peter holding two keys; over the head of each an estoile, over the keys a quatrefoil. In the base under a trefoil S. Eadburga, three-quarter length, in the right-hand a chalice, in the left an open book; on each side an estoile.[2]

Dugdale[3] shows a seal somewhat different—possibly a later copy of this one.

ii. A somewhat indistinct cast of a 13th Cent. counter seal, pointed oval shape, about 1⅝in. × 1⅛in. broad. Inscribed—

Seal No. i.

✠ SIGIL'M · SC̄E · MARIE · ET · SC̄ · EADBURGE VIRG · PSOR.

It shows the Virgin with crown, turned to the right, seated on a throne; in her arms the Child with a beaded nimbus; before her kneels S. Eadburga adoring.

iii. Attached to the documents acknowledging the supremacy of Henry VIII. is a seal which "shows S. Eadburga holding a chalice and a book veiled."[4]

Seal No. ii.

iv.[5] A cast imperfect and indistinct of a 13th Cent. seal of Roger de Radeby, 1234-1249 (51?); it is of pointed oval form, 2¼in. long by 1⅜in. broad, showing the Abbot full length, holding in his right hand a pastoral staff and in his left a book. The inscription is partially defaced:—

✠ SIGILL' · RO . . . · DEI · GR̄A . . . BATI · PERSORE ·

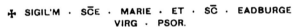

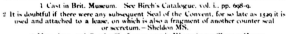

𝒙

Seal No. iii.

1 Cast in Brit. Museum. See Birch's Catalogue, vol. i., pp. 698-9.
2 It is doubtful if there were any subsequent Seal of the Convent, for so late as 1529 it is used and attached to a lease, on which is also a fragment of another counter seal or secretum.—Sheldon MS.
3 Mon. Aug., vol. ii., pl. xiii., from a cast in Westminster Chapter House.
4 Walcot ex. Pratt. MSS., vol. xxvii.
5 Cast in Brit. Mus.

The following is a list of the Abbots, and notes concerning them, compiled from various authorities, and as consecutive as existing record makes possible :--

984 A.D. FOLDBRITH[1] (whose name is also given as Foldbright, Folbert, Fulbert, Floberht, and Ealdbright), the first Benedictine Abbot. Installed by Oswald, Bishop of Worcester. Died August 2nd, 988. Of him is related the legendary story of resuscitation. There is a portrait panel of about this date built into the exterior of the south aisle wall of Beoley Church, Worcestershire (in which district Pershore had considerable possessions), and it has been supposed by some to be of this Abbot and to relate to the legend.

——— BRICTHEGE (or BRITHEAG). The date of his election, or if there were any Abbot between him and Foldbrith, is unknown, but in 1032 he witnessed Canute's Charter to Croyland.[2] In 1033 he was raised to the Bishopric of Worcester.[3] He died in 1038.[3]

1034 ——— The immediate successor of Bricthege is not recorded.

1044 ALFRIC.[4]

——— ROGER. Died in 1074.[4]

1074 (?) EADMUND. He is mentioned in the Domesday, and also he is recorded to have attended the Council of London in 1082 ; and died on June 23rd, 1085.

1085 TURSTAN (TURSTIN or THURSTAN). A monk of Gloucester. Died 1087.[5]

1087 GUIDO (or WIDO). Deposed by Anslem, at the Council of Westminster, in 1102.[6] Some have said because he was a foreigner, and others, and more correctly, for Simony. At this Council several others —English as well as " francigenae " -were also deposed, and on the same account. He died 1137,[7] and from the Annals of Tewkesbury it would appear that he must have been restored, and was Abbot at the time of his death ; if this were not so the records clash.

1138 WILLIAM.[8] A monk of the cell of Eye.

1140 THOMAS.[9] Died 1161.

1162 REGINALD. Died 1174.[10]

1170 ROGER. Died 1174.[10] There is some doubt about this name. Reginald is not stated to have resigned, and with the date of his death given in the Annals of Tewkesbury his successor, Symon, is stated as for the next year, yet the Annals of Worcester state Roger, Abbot of Pershore, as having died in 1174. I think the solution may best be found in accepting the names of Reginald and Roger for one and the same man.

1175 SYMON[11] (SIMON DE AMBRESLEY). Died at Bermondsey, May 12th, 1198.[12]

1198 ANSELM.[13] A monk of Reading ; blessed at Worcester, to which he sent four marks as a pittance. Died 1203.

1203 SIMON.[14] Confirmed on All Saints' Day at Worcester.

1204 GERVASE[15] (or GILBERT). Received blessing at Worcester ; died 1234 on Easter Day. He carried out the beautiful 13th Cent. work of the present Choir after the fire in 1223.

1 Ann. Wig., W. de Malms, Leland Coll., etc.   2 Hist. Ingulphi.

3 Hoveden, also Florence of Worc., who says he was nephew of Wulfstan, Archbishop of York.

4 Nash, Willis, etc.   5 Hoveden.   6 Hoveden ; W. of Malms.

7 Ann. Theok.   8 Florence of Worc.   9 Cole MS.

10 Ann. Wig., Ann. Theok., Florence.   11 Ann. Theok.   12 Ann. Wig., Ann. de Winstonia., Ann. Theok.

13 Ann. Wig., Ann. Theok , Florence.   14 Stevens Cont., Willis.

15 Ann. Theok., Ann. Wig., etc.

1234 ROGER DE RADEBY[1] (or RUDELEY). A Monk of Pershore ; blessed at Worcester, and paid fees for cope and alb and 40s. for procuration ; died 1249. Annals of Worcester give his death in 1251 ; if so he must have resigned his Abbacy at the earlier date. During his rule S. Andrew's Church was appropriated. A cast of his seal is in the British Museum, and a reproduction is given above.

1249 (March 19th) ELER (or ELFRIC). A Monk of Fécamp ; Prior of Cogges, Oxon. Resigned October 24th, 1262. He, together with the Abbot of Glastonbury, presided at a General Chapter of Benedictines held at Evesham in 1254.[2] In 1255 he collected money in Wales for a crusade. He was made Escheater of all England by Henry III. in 1262.[3] During his Abbacy the Lady Chapel was completed.

1263 (Nov. 12th) HENRY DE BIDEFORD[4] (or BEDFORD). He was summoned to Parliament.[5]

1274 (Dec. 3rd) HENRY DE CALDEWELL.[6] Sacrist of Pershore. Died at his Manor at Lege, March 6th, 1289.[7]

1289 (March 12th) WILLIAM DE LEGE, Cellarer of the House. Blessed at Urthenden.[8] Summoned to Parliament in 1295 and again in 1299. In 1294 the King, Edward I., was guest at the Abbey.

About 1299, during the rule of this Abbot, or between his and that of the next, some trouble occurred in the House, and the services in the Church were suspended, but at length reconciliation was effected by the interposition of the Bishop of Llandaff.[9]

1304 (June 5th) WILLIAM DE HERVINGTON[10] (HERWYNTON or KERVINGTON). Resigned 1340. Probably the sepulchral effigy of an Abbot now existing in the Church is of him.[11]

1340 (Nov. 21st) THOMAS DE PYRTON,[12] Cellarer of the House. Died July 3rd, 1358.[13] Edward III. borrowed 100 marks of this Abbot in 1346 and some wool for his French wars.

1349 (Aug. 30th) PETER DE PENDOCK. Resigned August 8th, 1363.

1363 (Sep. 23rd) PETER DE BRADWEY[14] (or BRADEWEYE).

1379 (Nov. 17th) THOMAS UPTON.[15] Said to have been drowned in crossing the Avon during flood in 1413, after which disaster the monks are said to have built the bridge. During his Abbacy the Churches of Eckington, Broadway, and S. Peter's at Worcester were appropriated to the Abbey.

1 Angl. Sac., Florence of Worc.   2 Ann. Theok., Florence of Worc.
3 Pat. 35 Henry III.   4 Pat. 49 Henry III.
5 Pershore was a mitred Abbey, and its Abbot was entitled to sit in Parliament.
6 Pat. 3 Ed. I.   7 Ann Wig., Florence.
8 Florence ; Ann. Wig., and on account of the recent injury of the Monastery by fire some expenses were excused. *ibid.*
9 A.D. 1299, in cal. Julij. Johannes episcopus Landavensis reconciliavit ecclesiam Persorensem, quia custos ecclesiae muliebri consilio infatuatus in loco illo sacrato ignem obtulit alienum."—Ann. Wig.
10 Pat. 35 Ed. I.
11 Willis makes a mistake in supposing the brass of Sir Adam de Hewington to be "the gravestone of this Abbot," and his explanation of the error in the name is perfectly foolish. See page 26.
12 Pat. 14 Ed. III.
13 Pratt. MS. ; this being so he must have resigned in 1349, nine years previous to his death.
14 Pat. 17 Ed III., which mentions Pendock also.
15 Pat. 1 Rich. II.

1413 (June 3rd) WILLIAM DE NEWNTON.[1] Died February 14th, 1450. His rebus is on one of the shields on the bosses of the south transept vaulting and is—in the chief, " W. Newn," in the base a tun with a chain extending.

1450[2] . . . . . .

1456 (April 22nd) EDMUND HERT.[3] Resigned April 15th, 1479, and on his death was buried in the Abbey ; Habington considers the effigy to be his.

1479 (April 26th) ROBERT STANWAY.[4] Buried in the Abbey.

1497 (Aug. 27th) JOHN PYBLETON[5] (PEOPLETON). Died 1504.

1504 (March 25th) WILLIAM COMPTON.[6] A Monk of Tewkesbury. The Church at Mathon was appropriated in 1512.[7] The rebus of this Abbot was *or*, a tun, on a chief *sable* the letter " W," and a comb of the first.[8] He probably resigned before his death.[9]

1527 (Oct. 16th) JOHN STONEWELL[10](or STANGWELL), D.D. Prior of Gloucester Hall, Oxford. He bequeathed some of his personal property to the Church of St. James, Longdon, attached to which he had a chantry, wherein he was buried in July, 1553. He was Suffragan Bishop under the title " Poletensis," using which he signed the documents of Henry's supremacy in 1534.[11] His arms were -sa, between three wells on a chevron *or*, three leaves proper ; on a chief of the second a crown *gu* between two parrots.

---

1 Pat. 1 Henry V. Willis is in error as to the date here. he gives it 1434, reading the inscription on an old panel as the date of the election of this Abbot. See page 28.
2 Willis says Newnton lived till 1456, and continued Abbot until his death.
3 Pat. 35 Henry VI.   4 Pat. 19 Edw. IV.   5 12 Henry VII.
6 Kennett MS.   7 Nash Coll.   8 Pratt. MS.
9 A paper in the Augmt. Off. is entitled "Answer of John, Abbot of Pershore, to the complaint of William Compton, late Abbot there."
10 Pat. 18 Henry VIII.   11 Pratt. MS

13th Cent. Tiles.

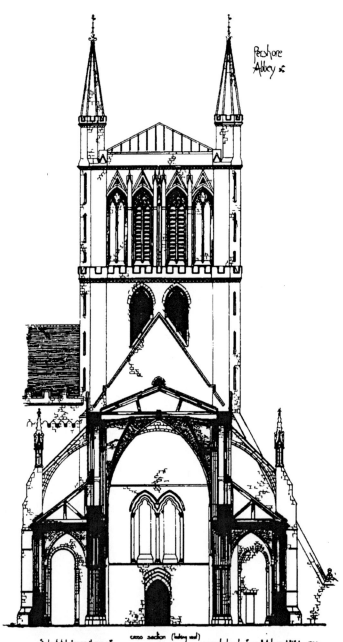

Pershore
Abbey &c

cross section (looking east)

Scale of feet   measured & drawn by James B Andrews A. R.Ibbly 1904.

PART II.—OF THE MONASTIC BUILDINGS, ETC.

OF the buildings of the Monastery as a whole no very certain account can be given, for so much has been destroyed or defaced ; but a considerable portion of the general plan has been discovered by excavation undertaken at various times. In some cases, however, the original foundations have been removed, and in others later buildings having been erected upon them, their earlier form and arrangement has been obliterated ; parts of the plan, therefore, must be left to conjecture.

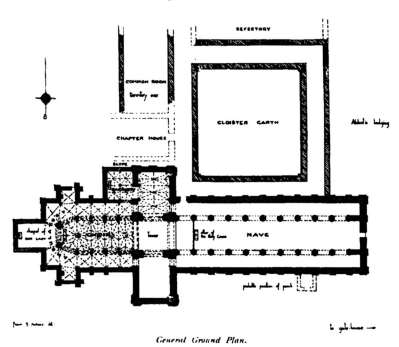

General Ground Plan.

The Precinct included about ten acres, and the arrangements were on the customary lines of a Benedictine Monastery.

The Cloister occupied the usual position on the south side of the Church ; it was about 100 feet square, and was entered from the Nave, in the south-east bay of which, adjoining the transept, there remains a doorway of 13th Cent. work, having clustered jambs, carrying a richly-moulded arch of beautiful proportion[1] ; near this entrance, and on the cloister side of it, is a small aumbry.

The position of the Fratery, the Chapter House (of oblong plan), the Common Room or Parlour (with the dormitory over), and the Slype, and the location of the Abbot's Lodge, Gatehouse,[2] and Entrance Archway[3] (and probably adjoining this the Almonry), are the only other parts of the plan of which there is anything like certain knowledge.

The present house known as "The Abbey," which stands on the site of the buildings that adjoined the western side of the Cloister, no doubt includes some of the original work, particularly in its substructure.

There are portions of a moat still to be found.

A Vineyard occupied a considerable portion of Allesborough Hill, about half a mile distant ; Orchards are also referred to, and Fish Ponds.

The Monks' Cemetery lay in an easterly direction, perhaps in part where now is the churchyard of S. Andrew's.

Cloister Doorway.

THE CHURCH.—The remaining fragments of the Church of Pershore Abbey exhibit examples of each period of mediæval architecture, from Early Norman down to the latest development of Gothic ; and while this is not a remarkable occurrence in itself, for very many less extensive Churches do so also, yet in this instance it has exception on account of the peculiar beauty of the work. If but the Norman Nave still stood, Pershore would be able to claim examples of three periods, practically successive -of special remark and magnificence. The Norman work yet existing is in the Transept and crossing ; it is of early date. possibly parts of the Transept are even pre-Norman ; the details are noteworthy—the very lofty arches of the crossing, the internal wall arcading of the Transept, and the interlacing arcade in the gable on the exterior. Early English work, of the first quarter of the 13th Cent., is represented in the Choir Arcade and superstructure, and exhibits a specimen of considerable rarity and beauty, so much so that no example at all comparable to it exists in the county, nor is one to be

1 Above which, hidden in the ivy, are fragments of a window.
2 Dugdale said it was still remaining.
3 This lofty archway existed about 1830, when on account of its ruinous condition it was pulled down. It stood just about where the gateway outside the north gate of the churchyard now stands. At this time some other fragments were also cleared away.

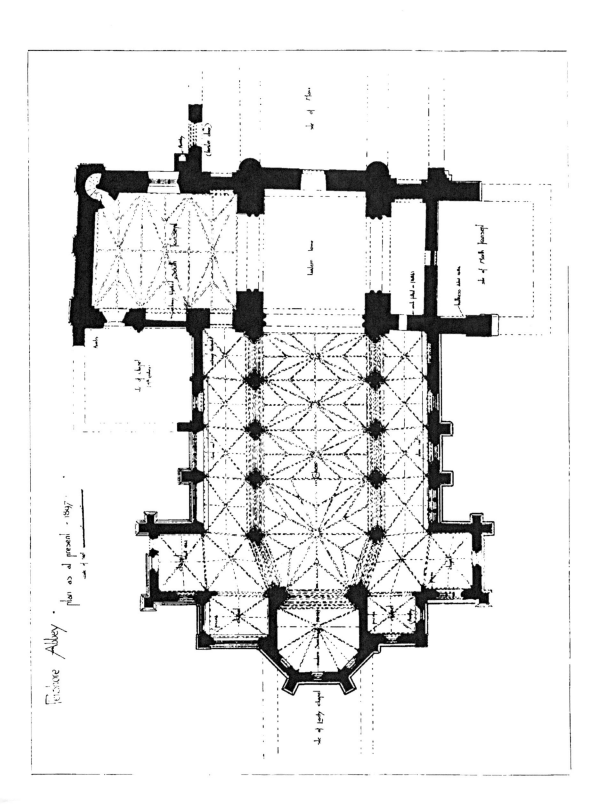

Pershore Abbey . plan as at present . 1897 .

easily produced elsewhere that will better exhibit the detail of the period. The chief instance of Decorated work—14th Cent.—is to be found in the Lantern Tower, an example difficult, if at all possible, to equal, and certainly not to excel, in all England. Of this period, too, is the vaulting of the main roof of the Choir and South Transept. Later periods also are represented, but only by smaller details, which do not call for any special note.

THE NAVE.—Of the Nave, foundations have been discovered showing it to have consisted of ten bays, about 180 ft. in total length and 60 ft. in width, built in Norman (or *Romanesque*) style of architecture, early in the 12th Cent.

It was of great similarity[1] to those of the sister Churches at Gloucester (*date 1089-1100 A.D.*) and Tewkesbury (*1103-1120 A.D.*), and the builders were probably associated with each other, and possibly under the same general directions; Gloucester being executed first, then Tewkesbury and Pershore both about the same period. Each building has the same massive round piers,[2] with shallow cushion caps and plain semi-circular arches, with triforia and clerestories considerably compressed on account of the peculiarly lofty proportions of the arcades beneath.

Only the responds to the west of the crossing and a fragment of one bay on the north side still stand. The western arches of the tower and aisles were blocked up at the time of the demolition of the Nave, and the doorway and two-light windows over it, now in existence, replaced others inserted at or soon after the closing of those arches—the present were part of the restorations of 1862. Some fragments of finely-tapering pinnacles have been lately discovered, which suggest the lines of those of the western turrets of Tewkesbury—and it may have been that Pershore's Nave had a somewhat similar termination at its west end.

THE TRANSEPT.—The Transept was about 160 ft. long and 40 ft. wide. The northern portion is said to have fallen in the 17th Cent., and to take its place in supporting the Tower a long raking buttress was erected.[3]

The work of the remaining portion, the south, is of a very early period, having large joints and ornamental details and mouldings of characteristic design. It has been said to be a part of Oddo's work shortly previous to the Norman Conquest, and probably part of the lower portion is pre-Norman. On the west side is a window inserted in the 15th Cent. of similar style, and executed about the same time as others in the south aisle of the Choir. High up in the south gable is some interlacing arcading, below which is a plain triplet lancet window of Early English period, and to the east and west walls are corbel tables with grotesquely-carved heads. On a level with the window, and also below it, in the interior, are small round-arched arcades, screening passages in the thickness of the wall, continuing along the east side, and connecting with the triforium passage of the Choir; some of the shafts and caps of these arcades and the string molds and other details are enriched with chevrons and carvings. On the south and part of the east walls is a base arcade, originally having shafts and caps, all of which are gone, and it shows considerable evidence of fire damage. The groined vault is of early 15th Cent. work; the rebus of Abbot Newnton (1413-50), the crossed keys of S. Peter and other devices on heater-shaped shields enrich some of the bosses and corbels.[4]

1 Walcot.
2 A fragment of one of the caps gives a diameter for its pier. of 6 ft.
3 This buttress bears the following inscription in two panels on the finial at the base :-"William Yend, John Marriott, Church-wardens. This buttress was erected in 1686. John Clark, Minister."
4 The charges of the various shields are as follows :-Party per pale, three cups, a chief dancette. two lions as supporters ; a heart-shaped shield ducally crowned with two W's interlacing with two transverse bars ; two wyverns with one head ; two keys saltier-wise ; the cross of S. George ; and the rebus of Abbot Newnton. In no instance is there any indication of the tinctures.

Dr. King remarks on the staircase in the south-west angle that it has peculiarity in projecting in the interior of the building, the more usual course being to extend external turrets beyond the thickness of the walls as required for the stair-way, or to confine them within the wall thickness itself. He also refers to the enrichment of the base arcade, and says it is of "diamond work manifestly of such a kind as one would take them rather to have been meant for a lady's pattern for needlework than for an architect's design in building."

THE TOWER.—The Lantern Tower is of early 14th Cent. work; it measures about 40 ft. square externally and 30 ft. internally. It stands on four lofty Norman arches, springing from massive piers, faced on each side with coupled attached three-quarter shafts, having cushion caps, most of which are scolloped and enriched, but that at the south-west angle has figure subjects of some elaboration.[1] These arches doubtless bore the tower, destroyed by the fire in 1288 A.D., and as about half a century after that fire the tower was spoken of as being in ruins, 1335 A.D. will approximate very nearly the date when the present superstructure was commenced and shortly after completed. It rises to a height of 60 ft. above these arches, which makes the total from the ground about 116 ft., and to the top of the modern pinnacles 144 ft. Externally, the upper or belfry storey, divided from the lower by an embattlemented band (a very rare feature at this period), exhibits on each face four canopied arches, slightly recessed behind the angle stair turrets, and divided by square pilaster shafts, which occur in pairs in the middle of each face. The two central arches on each face are pierced for light, the others are blank, and all have mullions and traceried heads; the lantern storey has on each side two traceried windows of two lights, the lower portions of which are shut off by the weather molds of the roofs of the choir and transepts, which rise obliquely on either face. The turrets of the stair are now crowned with modern pinnacles (added in 1870 by Mr. Scott), but originally they rose only just above the parapet. There exists to the north-east angle of the tower a semi-classic buttress (dated 1686), which was erected when, not having the support of the north transept, the tower was considered somewhat unsafe.

Internally it has an exceedingly beautiful and unique lantern storey.[2] Of it Mr. Scott said, "I hardly know of a lantern storey so beautiful as that of Pershore; it stands, so far as I know, quite alone in its design."

It is richly panelled and traceried, and is pierced in the thickness of its walls by two narrow passages, one above the other; from the upper of these passages access is made to the modern ringing stage, which has been so arranged as to interfere as little as may be with the view of the lantern from the floor below.

The mouldings of the walls were once decorated with colour, of which traces still remain, and, being intended to be viewed from below, the lower surfaces of them only were coloured.

The Belfry contains eight bells,[3] one of the finest peals in the country, though surpassed by some of larger size and number; the tenor weighs about 1½ tons, and gives the note D♮. The

---

1 King says, illustrative of the trial of Susanna before David.—*Mun. Antiq.*
2 Scott said also, "with the single exception of Lincoln Cathedral, probably the most beautiful of its class to be found in any English Church."
3 They come from Abraham Ruddal's foundry in Gloucester, and bear the following mottoes:—
    TENOR.—"I to the Church the living call;
        And to the grave do summon all."
    7TH.—"Richard Roberts, Esq., John Yeend, and Thomas Ashfield, gentlemen, trustees. A.R. 1729."
    6TH.—"Walter Marriott, and Edmund Cole, churchwardens. 1729."
    5TH.—"Prosperity to all our benefactors. A.R. 1729."
    4TH.—"Prosperity to the Church of England" (cracked).
    3RD.—"Abraham Ruddall, of Gloucester, cast all of us."
    2ND.—"Peace and good neighbourhood."
    TREBLE.—"Joseph Martin, and Thomas Evans, churchwardens. 1814."
During 1897 they have been rehung, and the cracked 4th recast by J. Barwell & Sons, with moderate success.

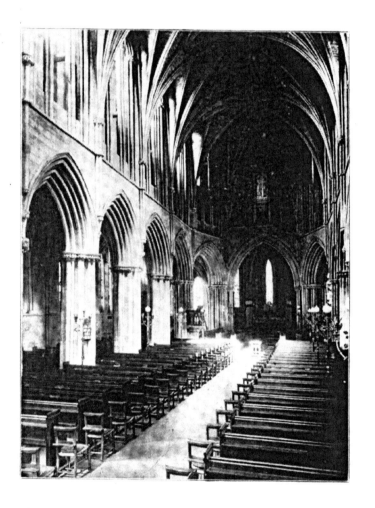

Pershore Abbey.   Interior of the Choir.

original floor, being considered unsafe, was replaced in 1836; the timber roof over is not the original one, it is of considerable age, but its date is not known.

Apart altogether from its intrinsic beauty and rarity, there is a most remarkable and note-worthy incident connected with this Lantern Tower; it is in the distinct analogy existing between it and that of the Cathedral of Salisbury; so far, indeed, does this similarity extend that it includes some special features of rare and unusual disposition.

To describe the later building, Pershore, requires practically nothing more than a reiteration of the description of the earlier. At Salisbury the main work was carried out between the years of 1220 and 1256 A.D., and included the lower or lantern stage of the Central Tower (the present vaulting cutting this off from below being a later addition); on the exterior this stage receives the four abutting roofs of the crossing, and on the interior is divided in the wall thickness with a passage having a shafted and arcaded front; each angle of the tower is pierced with a stair, and is of peculiar form in plan, projecting slightly and square to the main wall face and having its exterior angle splayed off as if part of an octagon; with this stage the 13th Cent. work at Salisbury was completed, and on this, in 1330 A.D., the two upper stages were raised, which were culminated with the lofty and beautiful spire between 1335 and 1370 A.D.

At Pershore, however, there was no break in the work, the lantern and its superstructure were carried out continuously; the remaining ruin of the earlier tower—whatever that may have been, probably Norman—was cleared away down to the string mold directly over the 12th Cent. arches of the crossing, and from this point the lantern and belfry stages were raised,

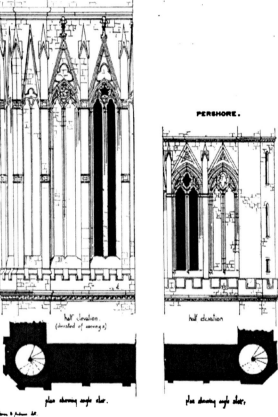

Sketch Elevations of the Exterior of Salisbury and Pershore Towers.

commencing, probably, about 1335 A.D. As at Salisbury, here also is a precisely similar form of plan: the stair turrets are identical: the exterior treatment of the façades of the belfry stage correspond exactly, though divested of the carved enrichments of the former: the flat pilaster-shafts dividing the blank and pierced arches on each face and coupled in the centre, are alike:

so, also are the canopies to the arcades; while the embattlemented cornice-band to the lantern stage is remarkable in both instances, apart from the connection, on account of the exceptionally early date at which it occurs. In many other minor details, also, is there continuing analogy to be found.

The designs of the interior elevations of the lanterns are not, however, to be compared; that of Pershore is far more beautiful than that of Salisbury, and no later vaulting exists to obscure it from view from the floor of the crossing; it forms, probably, the finest example of its kind in the kingdom, certainly there is no Church of equal size in which anything comparable to it exists.

As to this parallelism, the only interpretation must lie in the fact that the architect of Salisbury designed, and probably directed, the execution of the Pershore work also. After careful study of the two structures no other conclusion can well be arrived at; nor is this explanation difficult of credence; it is far easier than to believe that two distinct minds could ever have travelled, the one after the other, so far and so regularly along a similar path of thought, and have produced, without contact, designs so alike both in their *motif* and in their detail; and also it would be difficult to believe such an unprecedented course was adopted by the Pershore workmen as to copy simply the Salisbury work, amending it to date as they went on.

This explanation in the identity of the architect, although his name has been unfortunately lost in the obscurity of the ages, is, after all, the only feasible one, the one upheld by Sir Gilbert Scott and the Rev. Mackenzie E. Walcott, and may well be accepted except for the lack of that proof, which probably will never now be produced   absolute historic statement.

THE CHOIR.—The present Choir was the work of Abbot Gervase in the 13th Cent., and was consecrated in 1239 A.D.; it is a splendid specimen of Early English architecture, peculiarly beautiful, and very unusual in its design. It consists of four straight bays on either side, and one returning at an angle toward the eastern arch (which is wider than the rest), and forms a peculiar apsidal termination almost exactly on the lines of that of Tewkesbury.

The bays of the arcade consist of richly-moulded arches,[1] springing from lozenge-shaped piers, which have at their angles attached triple shafts, which repeat in the centre of each face and occasionally alternate with larger single shafts, rising from richly-moulded bases and terminating in beautiful foliated and moulded caps. The piers of the eastern arch are enriched with detached slate and Purbeck marble shafts, four inches in diameter, cramped with peculiar secret iron cramps to the piers, and bear such resemblance to those of Worcester Cathedral that Mr. Walcott supposed them to have been executed by the same school of masons.

The triforium and clerestory merge in lofty triplets extending from just above the ground arcade to the vaulting, and externally have single lancets of very simple design.

Springing of East and South-east Arches of Choir.

---

1 For details see plate of mouldings.

Pershore Abbey.

Scale of feet

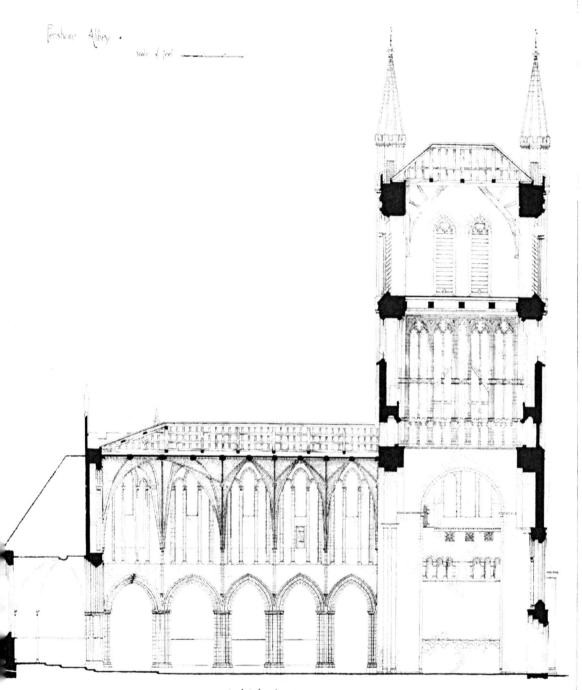

longitudinal section (looking south)

measured & drawn by John H. Jackson F.R.I.B.A. 1899

The main roof is formed by a rich stellar vault at a height of 60 ft. from the floor; it is of about the same date as the Lantern Tower. It springs from triplet vaulting shafts, which are continued down to carved corbels in the spandrils of the arcade below, and has large and very delicately carved bosses and richly moulded main and lierne ribs. Above is a cambered timber and lead roof of later date, but the weather mold of the earlier one of sharp pitch may be seen on the Tower face. On the exterior it is buttressed with graceful flying buttresses[1] on each side, and has an embattlemented parapet with crocketted pinnacles of later date carried on a pointed corbel table. The aisles have simple quadripartite vaulting of earlier date, and are covered in with modern tile roofs.

It is probable that the work of this period was erected on the foundations of that of the former choir, for the apsidal ending is not only rare, but is not here correctly set out[2] (the expedient to cover which inaccuracy by a graceful bunch of carved foliage to receive the mouldings is an interesting point at the springing of the east and south-east arches). At Tewkesbury, where the lines of the plan are the same as here, the Norman piers remain.

The window of the extreme east bay of the north aisle is a shafted triplet,[3] enclosed under a larger arch externally. This window possibly was inserted after the completion of the general work, as it is the only one of early date that differs from the general treatment; the other bays have single lancets, and all are moulded and shafted internally with plain chamfered orders on the exterior. The windows of the two eastern bays of the south aisle have been replaced with late Decorated, or Early Perpendicular insertions of five lights each to make up the light lost when the erection of the Sacristy blocked out the lancets of the two adjoining bays toward the west.

At the ends of the aisles, and breaking from them north and south (like small transepts and similar to those at Worcester and Rochester), are chapels of about the same period as the rest of the work of the Choir. The Lady Chapel[4] at the east end (long since destroyed) was probably also of a similar style; the bases of its walls were about 5 ft. thick, and at a distance of 50 ft. east of the Choir, part have been traced— about 4 ft. below the existing ground line; the present erection is modern, and of quite inferior design. The south chapel was practically rebuilt in 1862, the fragments that remained being too ruinous for restoration. It contained a piscina, and is said to have had an aumbry. Piscinas are also to be found on the east wall of the north chapel, and in the north-east on its south wall (this having a trefoil arched head), and also an aumbry on the north side of this chapel, opposite which, built into the masonry which now blocks up the Ambulatory arch, is another plain-arched piscina.

CHAPELS AND CHANTRIES.—There is considerable and almost conclusive evidence that the Transepts here had, as at Tewkesbury and elsewhere, apsidal eastern chapels of early date; there exists a wide arch in the south transept which evidently opened originally into such a chapel,[5] and this is exactly as at Tewkesbury, even to the high triforium arch over it. Probably the chapel was pulled down and the arch blocked up in the 14th Cent. to allow for the construction of the larger Sacristy, of which so very distinct traces remain, and evidence

---

1 The pinnacles of these buttresses are entirely modern, and there was no exact precedent for their present design.

2 The Norman Choir was destroyed probably by the fire in 1223; other inaccuracies may be found, and in the spacing of the piers of arcades variations up to 3 ft. 3½ in.

3 See detail.

4 In 1259 A.D. the Lady Chapel is recorded as not then complete, but it was probably nearly so. Styles (1838) refers to remains of such, and as being a little later in date than the Choir; these remains must have been removed in 1846 for the erection of the present sanctuary, when a partial restoration was carried out, previous to which the richly-moulded and shafted eastern arch was blocked up; against it the altar then stood, above which almost filling up the tympanum of the arch, was a huge royal coat of arms. And at this time a cottage, which was built against the south-east Chapel, was pulled down.

5 The lines of the roof may be easily distinguished on the exterior of the east wall of the Transept.

External Arcade on South Transept Wall.

a structure of considerable beauty. The vaulting of this Sacristy, extending two bays each way, must have been supported with a moulded central pier—a rare and beautiful feature. This chapel was entered from the Choir by an archway inserted in the western bay of the south aisle. Let into the wall of the south transept is a richly-carved, moulded, and canopied wall-arcade of three bays, in date about the later half of the 14th Cent.; it stands on a low plinth course, which was doubtless a seat originally; continuing beyond these, and broken forward about 12 in., is a fourth bay, but of much earlier date—the later part of the 13th Cent. and of greater richness of moulding and tracery, and beneath it is an aumbry. From this last detail of late Early English period (*Geometrical*) must be argued the existence of some building of that date abutting at this end at least of the south transept, for it certainly was not a mere external wall enrichment; what building, and how extensive, it is hard to say, it must, however, have been of some importance, for work of the same date extends high above this ground bay, and is embedded in the modern buttress which strengthens the angle of the transept; it may have been an earlier Sacristy.[1]

Arcade. east wall of South Transept

Plan

1 I find Mr. Scott refers to this also, and suggests an eastern aisle to the transept; I do not think this probable, for there is no trace of its abutment on the south wall of the Choir, nor any other sign of its existence, nor do I think it at all likely that an aisle would have been added in such a position.

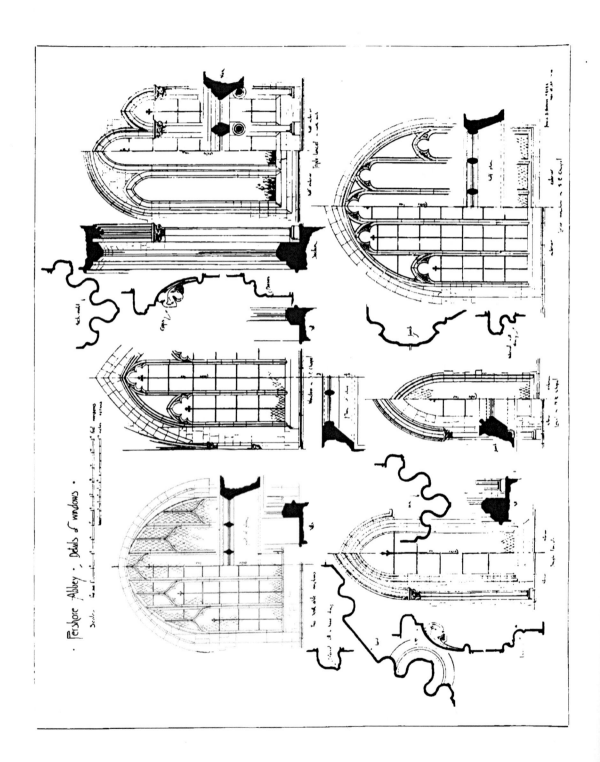

Pershore Abbey . Details of windows .

A Chapel of St. John the Baptist also existed, and a Chapel in the town dedicated to St Michael is mentioned.

There is an apartment, now forming a cellar under some premises in High Street, containing a 14th Cent. piscina, and bearing other evidences of having been used for religious purposes. The walls are some 6ft. thick, and it has a vaulted ceiling ; if it were a chapel it must have been of very late institution, for fragments of the 13th Cent. moulded stonework and other of later periods, even to the 15th Cent., were used in its construction, and probably had been taken from the Abbey. Above it was originally a large hall about 40ft. long, with a circular staircase to approach this chapel (?) below.

THE MONUMENTS. -

   i. The most important monument, and the oldest, is that of a Knight Templar. The effigy shows a Knight of 13th Cent. date[1] now placed on a large stone coffin of later date. It has been moved at various times to different parts of the Church and Churchyard whence it was last rescued—and now lies in the South

The Crusader's Effigy.

Transept. Speaking of it, Habington says : " In the north side of the quyre, somewhat raysed from the ground lyeth the portrature of a Knight of the holy voyage, armed all in mayle saveing his face, and right hand upon a hunter's horne depending from his belt ; on his left arme his sheild, the extreame and lowest end whereof a serpent byteth ; over his armour a military coat gyrt, a sword by his side, the legges are crossed and at his feete a hare. It is a received tradition that his name was Hareley, sometyme lord of a place in this parish called Hareley."

---

1 1250 A.D. Bloxam.

The hauberk in which the figure is attired is short-sleeved and hooded, and the lappel is unlaced at the neck and thrown back, showing the method of fastening; the rings are interlacing and set edgeways; over the mail is a surcoat, belted. The legs are crossed just below the knee, and now are broken off a little lower down.

There are several points of special rarity and interest in this monument, and these the late M. H. Bloxam discussed in a paper he read to the Archæological Institute,[1] and particularly on the special detail of the horn[2] held in the right hand of the effigy, from which he concluded that it evidenced that the Knight held his land by cornage tenure or "horn geld." Various statements have been made as to the resting of the feet, one has said on a hare—and deduced therefrom the name of the knight as Hareley,[3] another a Wyvern,[4] and a third and probably most correctly—on a lion couchant.[5]

Abbot Hervington's Tomb.

Dean Spence thinks it was Sir Wm. de Harley, Lord of Harley, in Shropshire, who fought in the first Crusade, and was knighted, so tradition says, by Godfrey de Bouillon at Jerusalem.

ii. The mutilated effigy of an Abbot,[6] with the head resting on a mitre, signifying his resignation of office previous to death, which at least two of Pershore's Abbots did, and of whom it is supposed to be of William de Hervington (1304-1340).

It lies on a small table tomb, which is enriched with quatrefoil panels, but it is doubtful whether it belongs to the same period as the effigy or that it originally bore it. The Abbot is tonsured, and vested in the alb and other ecclesiastical garments, and holds a book between his hands.

---

1 Proceedings, vol. xx., 198.
2 There are others in Wadworth Ch., Yorks., and in Newland Churchyard, Forest of Dean, but these effigies are in hunting attire. In France there is a military effigy with a horn, date about 1301 A.D.
3 Habington.   4 Pratt. MSS.
5 Dingley in his Hist. from Marble, part ii., shows a lion in his sketch.
6 The position of this has also been changed, as indeed that of nearly all the monuments have; it used to be in the north chapel of the Choir, where, when this building was used as a schoolroom, it suffered considerable defacement.

iii. A shafted and canopied monument, probably of early 17th Cent. date, bearing the arms and crest of the Haselwood family,[1] to whom it belonged. It is about 10ft. 4in. long, 9ft. 10in. high, and projects 2ft. 7in. ; on it lies a recumbent figure dressed in armour, at the feet of which kneels a man, in civilian, the dress of Elizabethan period, and at the head a woman, also kneeling ; the front of the base is enriched with panels and arabesques; the canopy is borne on slender black marble shafts, and has characteristic ornaments on its cornice and soffit. A small panel attached to the wall under the canopy should bear the inscription, and in a

The larger Haselwood Tomb.

The smaller Haselwood Tomb.

drawing in Nash's *Worcestershire* the name of 'Richard Haselwood' appears, despite the statement to the contrary in the same book. It is, however, blank now. Habington says this monument stood "in the south aisle by the quire," and it is now refixed against the west wall of the south transept.

iv. A smaller monument of very late 16th Cent. date or early 17th., now erected against the west wall of the remaining part of the north transept, also belonged to the Haselwood family. It is about 6ft. long and 11ft. high and of shallow projection ; the arched recess above the base once contained two kneeling figures[2] ; on the front, carved in relief, are the figures of ten children — three male and six female — and one in a cradle (a curious detail) ; all are kneeling, except one who stands turned forward, and

1 Of Wick-Warren according to the blazon. Nash said it was of Timothy Haselwood, who was buried in 1550, but this is surely wrong, as the monument is of so much later date.
2 Habington.

is laughing; over the cornice of the monument is an elaborately quartered coat and crest in a circular panel, and on the frieze is the following inscription :—

" FOVLCO HASELWOOD, ARMIGER   DOROTHEA VXORE · DICTI · FOVLCONIS
WHO VERTVE LOVING · VICE · REFRAIND   WHO WIDOWS POORE · AND · FATHERLESE
DISCORD ABHORING, PEACE MAINTAIND   ENTHRAWLD WᴴH WOOES · FREED FRŌ DISTRESSE
HIC IACET INVOLVTVS.   HÆC STATVA REP'SENTAT."

Records of interments of members of the Haselwood family are to be found in various places on the Church Registers up to about 1690.

v. The matrix of the brass is said to have lain on the floor of the south aisle; it was inscribed: "Sir Adam du Herwyngtone gyst ici Dev sa alme est mercy."[1] Its lettering was reported in 1838 to be fast wearing away, and no trace may now be discovered.

vi. Part of the arch, etc., of a late 15th Cent. tomb formed, previous to the last restoration, the head and jambs of a doorway into the North Chapel; on the

Fragment of a 15th Century Reredos (?) and the Chest.

fragments remaining are some conventional carvings, etc., of the period, and a panelled portion contains in one of its compartments an escutcheon charged with a hare *tripping* between three chalices or cups and the letters " B (or R) S."

vii. One or two stone coffins have been dug up, on the lid of one of which is a long cross fleury, and some sepulchral urns have also been discovered.[2]

x

---

1 Nash and others.
2 Dugdale and Nash. In 1793, when excavating for the enlargement of a vault in the Choir, a body was discovered, clothed, wearing a wig, and with a stake driven through it.—Nash. Suppl.

Other items of interest are :—

    i. A fine chest of early 15th or late 14th Cent. date ; it is 5ft. oin. by 2ft. 3½in. by 3ft. 2½in. high, and is massively panelled with fine traceries incised on the angle posts.

Pavement Tiles from the Abbey (reduced facsimiles).

    ii. In the floor of the South Chapel some 13th and 14th Cent. tiles are preserved, dug up in 1862 from the site of North Transept ; they were doubtless from the celebrated Malvern or Droitwich Kilns ; some bear heraldic and others conventional foliated decorations. In some of those charged with heraldic devices there appears to be an effort to indicate the blazon ; in the Episcopal bearings of the See of Worcester the buff colour of the tile is obviously intended to represent *or* and the terra-cotta *gules* for the ten torteaux ; also in the Beauchamp coat (1369-1401) *Gu.*, a fesse between six cross crosslets *or*; possibly also in one having the covered cups—the coat of Thomas Symonds, of White Ladies, Aston—*Sa.* three cups *arg.* covered *or*, whose coat this may (?) have been.

Pavement Tiles from the Cottage (reduced facsimiles).

In the floor of a cottage about a mile distant from the Abbey are a number of other tiles of about the same dates and with various other forms of decoration, among them the arms of England : three lions passant guardant, with a label of five points ; two keys saltier-wise with the letters "S. P. E." ; some of the tiles here are glazed and bear traces of colour.

iii. A small but elaborate fragment of woodwork, probably a portion of some parclose or screen. It is of the Perpendicular period, and bears this inscription—

> " 𝔐.ℭ. bis bino tripler ɼ abbere quarto
> Anno 𝔚illms bni 𝔑etwnton fect abbas."

It was, therefore, connected with some of the work of Abbot Newnton in 1434. It bears also the initials of Newnton, " W. N.," and " H. VI." (*Henry VI.*) " aᵒ xii." (*1434 A.D.*), and is traceried and carved. Nash speaks[1] of it as "new painted, gilded, and somewhat disfigured." It is the only piece of old woodwork—except some small parts of the stalls which are very plain - existing in the Church.

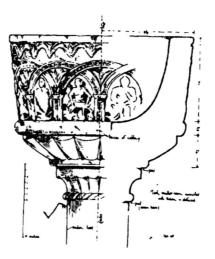

The original Norman Font.

iv. The Norman font is of extreme interest ; the original bowl still exists, but not in the Church, it is now in the grounds of "The Nash" at Kempsey, near Worcester, where it was taken shortly after the last restoration ; it is mounted on a modern pedestal. It is enriched with an interlacing arcade in the panels of which are figure subjects, but having been long exposed to the weather is much worn and encrusted with lichen.

v. Against the filling of the archway in the east wall of the South Transept is a fragment of 15th Cent. stonework which may have been either part of a reredos to an altar placed there when taken from the Chapel which stood originally on the site of the Sacristy, or it may have been the head of a screen dividing the Sacristy from the Transept previous to the blocking of the archway.

vi. The *Gentleman's Magazine*[2] shows a sketch of an interesting piece of Saxon brass-work, a shrine or reliquary, which was found when digging a cellar in the town.[3] Dr. King[4] describes it thus : " A small ornament of brass (*latten* probably), with a

1 In his account of the restoration in 1774. Dingley says it formed part of a screen to the north-east chapel of the Choir, which was then used as a school-house.—Hist. from Marble, pt. ii.
     2 Vol. xlxix.   3 Dug up in 1779. Beauties.   4 Mun. Antiq. 1805.

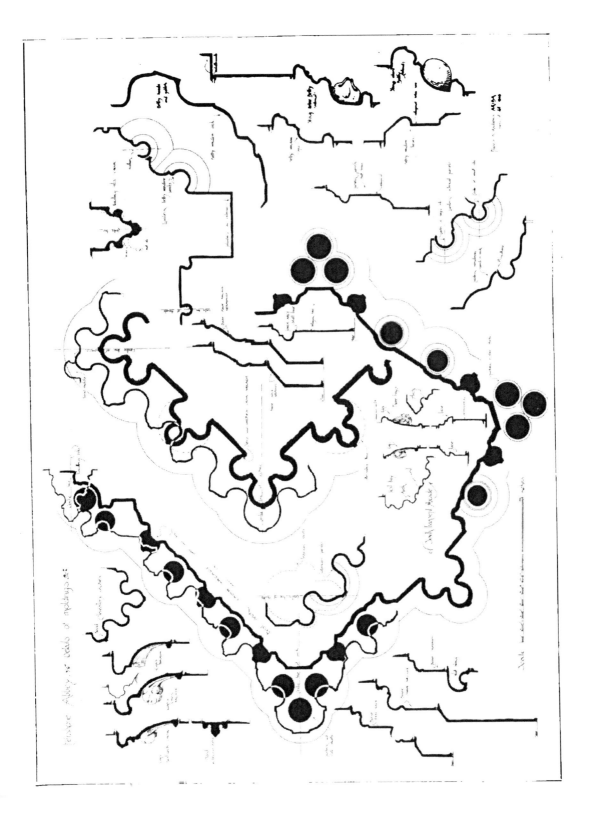

sort of filigree work, a little less than two inches square and four inches high, resembling a sort of rude dome, with odd rude heads of serpents and other kinds of animals, intermixed with the interlacing of the filigree, with some round Saxon arches also as a lower border, and with a rude Saxon inscription, 'Bodric me woth' *(Bodric me wrought)*, just over them.

It is hollow, and has at the four corners beneath four little pendant flaps (*these are fixed*) with holes, as if to nail it on some staff. And it seems, therefore, either to have been the head of a thick pastoral staff, or else of the top corner of a chair." What this really was is still somewhat doubtful; it probably was the upper part of a thurible.

vii. A somewhat elaborate 'S. John's Head' was said to have been discovered while excavating for the 1862 restorations. It is of alabaster, but much perished; the saint's head lies in a flat dish about 6¼ in diameter, with the hair hanging down on each side; on the dexter side is the figure of S. Peter, standing, and on the sinister an archbishop; above are two angels bearing the dish on which the head lies.[1]

viii. A small bronze crucifix was dug up about twenty-five years ago; it is

Saxon Thurible (?)
(From drawing in *The Gentleman's Magazine*, vol. xlxix.)

very well modelled, and its date probably late 15th Cent. This, the 'head,' and the brasswork are the only small articles of which I am aware that can be identified as once among the possessions of the Monastery.

x

THE RESTORATION.—At the time of the restoration in 1862 the walls inside the Church were thickly daubed with whitewash, high old-fashioned "box" pews occupied the floor, a gallery existed under the tower, and the lantern storey was entirely blocked out by a floor from which the bells were rung. The entrances were: From the west as now; from the north transept (to which there was a large modern porch); and also by a doorway in the present organ chamber. In the transepts, north and south, were partitions of lath and plaster, with monstrous quatrefoils and embattlemented cornices of abominable design. The floor generally was so raised by burials, etc., as to almost hide the pier bases; the building had been ruthlessly mutilated in the insertion of the fittings, etc., it then contained, and misjudged

---

efforts at repair had but caused further damage; indeed, as for the whole fabric, it was high time for a speedy and well-judged treatment, as in many places its ruinous condition was a source of imminent danger. The Restoration Committee retained the services of Sir Gilbert Scott, and on 10th November, 1862, the work was begun by Messrs. Collins & Co., of Tewkesbury, and completed in 1865, after the expenditure of some £6,000; in 1870 the pinnacles were added to the tower at a cost of £350, and in the two historic windows, the fresco work, etc., about £900 more is said to have been expended.

S. ANDREW'S.—The Church situated just outside the eastern wall of the present churchyard is dedicated to S. Andrew. The date of its founding was in the time of Edward the Confessor (Nash says much later—1147). It was erected to accommodate the tenants of Westminster, on account of bitterness of feeling between them and the Monks of Pershore, for, as already mentioned, Westminster had been given or had appropriated large parts of Pershore's property at various times. The Church was originally in the gift of the Prior and Monks of Malvern, but in 1241 A.D. it was granted to the Monastery, and this grant was confirmed again in 1327 A.D. It has been restored and rebuilt at various times, and the present structure is chiefly of 15th Cent. work.

Pershore held also other impropriate Churches—Mathon; S. Peter's, Worcester; Hawkesbury; Aldermaston, and Broadway.

THE BROADWAY GRANGE.—The Abbots of Pershore had a Grange[1] at Broadway, in Worcestershire. It was situated near the Green, and a considerable part still remains; the

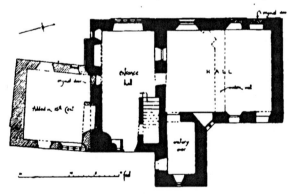

Ground Plan of Broadway Grange.

work is of the 14th Cent. date, and consists of three small stone buildings adjoining, but originally it must have been of much greater extent; in later times it has been altered and reältered to serve various modern purposes.

On the ground floor is an entrance hall, a hall proper, and a cellar, and on the upper floor the Abbot's room and a small oratory; to these has been added (about the middle of the 15th Cent.) other rooms abutting against the entrance hall on the south side. The present entrance possibly was the original one, but was probably then protected by a wooden porch; it leads into the somewhat low entrance hall, having a window at the opposite end, and in the

---

1 As well as the manor, which was sold in 1558 —Harl. MS.

side wall (next the hall) a door, with another door, a fireplace (the only original one in the building), and a small single-light cusp-headed window on the remaining side; the chimney is carried up on the exterior from the ground and high above is borne forward on plain stone corbels; the doorway by it has plain splayed jambs; to the right of the entrance is the staircase. The hall occupies the whole height of the building (it is now divided by a modern wall), and is covered in by a good open timber roof of the period; two windows of two lights each are in the walls of this apartment, and another, having a transom and a cusped head, is set angle-wise in the corner nearest the cellar, the original pivots of its shutters may be traced; and there are also two doorways (now built up), which probably led to the kitchen, buttery, etc.; breaking out towards the east is the block containing a cellar, with the oratory over. On the upper floor, over the entrance hall, is the Abbot's room, extending over the whole width, and covered with a good open timber roof; in the wall next the hall is a small window, or squint, down into the hall below; opposite is a doorway, now closed up; there are traceried windows of two lights in each end wall. The oratory—which is very small—adjoins, and it also has a little trefoil-headed window, or squint, into the hall, and a traceried two-light window at the east end, under which stood the altar. The 15th Cent. addition is at the south end, and consists of a ground floor apartment, with a room over, but has no features of remark.

The only private apartment is the Abbot's room; there can be no doubt that various domestic offices existed, although there is no trace of them now. The moat that surrounded the buildings was the only arrangement made for defence.

East Arch in South Transept.

Pershore Abbey, Worcestershire.

ADDENDA.

x

I.

CHARTER OF KING EADGAR.

972 A.D.

Translation of the Latin sentences [1] :--

✠
A
ꟃ

" By the admonition of ecclesiastical earnestness on the part of true believers we are frequently taught that in complete subjection we should worthily serve Him, Who, disposing the fabric of the whole world in wonderful and ineffable order, at length set down there most fittingly the microcosm, Adam to wit, moulded of the fourfold material, inspired by the gracious Breath into His own likeness, and placed him over all things which He had made in the world below, one thing alone for the sake of testing him being excepted and forbidden, with the delight of that charm of Paradise, Eve to wit, by his side as his helpmeet. But alas ! led away by the devilish sophistry of the cunning one, and enticed by the subterfuge of the persuasive female, the pair ate the forbidden apple, and, ejected into this calamitous world, earned for themselves and their successors perpetual death. For, as prophets foretell and put forth prognostications from heaven by the everlasting secret decree of the Exalted King, an angel, gloriously bringing down from on high a blessing on true believers, not as the factious loquacity of the Jews inelegantly professes, but compassing the most charming eloquence of ancients and moderns, by treading underfoot the Arian and Sabellian fables and making them of non-effect by his mystical utterances, and calling us from the blindness of thick gloom to the brightness of the inheritance on high, gliding forth from heaven's portals sang, 'tis said, into the ear of the undefiled Virgin, as the Gospel report sets forth, marvellous songs ; and the whole Catholic Church, crying aloud with consentient voice, acclaims her with him : ' Blessed art thou, the Virgin Mary, because thou hast believed that the things that were spoken unto thee by the Lord shall be performed in thee ! ' [2] And, wonderful to tell, the Word becomes flesh and is embodied, He, namely, of Whom the evangelist who excels in the depth of all his thoughts says : ' In the beginning was the Word, and the Word was with God, and the Word was God, etc.' [3] And by this incarnation spoken of, since it was assumed from the Virgin, the fault of the Virgin of old is removed, and honour bringing renown in shining splendours is bestowed on all women. Since, therefore, the sweet-savoured deity of Christ remained unimpaired, and His humanity suffered, liberty has become the lot of the slaves mercifully adjudged to Him.

Hence by the inspiration of the High-Throned One, I, Eadgar, King of the Angles and of the other tribes that dwell in the roads in wandering, [4] in order that I may deserve and obtain a share in this liberty by the mercy of the High-Throned Ruler, do grant a site for a convent at the renowned place which, by a noble name, is called Pershore by the peasants of that race ; and it shall be held dedicated to the Mother of our Lord, Mary the ever-virgin, and also to the Blessed Peter, chief of the apostles, and his fellow apostle Paul : [*I further grant*] perpetual liberty of monastic privilege to the monks living by rule, in so far as it existed after the decease of the celebrated Abbot Foldbriht, in whose times, by Christ's help, the restoration of this liberty was granted, whom the whole congregation of the aforesaid Monastery in due council had

---

1 Cott. MS. The complete copy of the Charter may be seen in facsimile in the British Museum Facs., vol. iii. 30., with a reprint of the sentences attached ; also see Birch Cart. Sax., vol. iii. Codex Dip. No. 570, and Earle's "Land Charters."
    2 cf Luke i. 45.   3 cf Jno i. 1.   4 Or ' round about.'

elected . . . . . . rightly selecting out of the same body of brethren may appoint. Moreover, the liberty of this privilege may be held in perpetual enjoyment by all Catholics, nor may anyone from outside, in bold reliance on tyrannical insolence, seize and exercise the right of power in the aforesaid Monastery, but the college of the same convent shall rejoice in the privilege of perpetual liberty, as I have said before.

But let the aforesaid Monastery be free of all land service on the same condition on which it had been released by our predecessor Coenulph, most earnest *defender* of the orthodox faith, as is contained in the ancient privilege, when Duke Beornoth obtained it.

Now the lands that have been granted for the use of the monks to our Lord Jesus Christ and Mary His Mother in ancient or modern times by kings and by religious persons of each sex and by myself in restoring the right, are the following, viz. :—In Perscoran (*Pershore*)[1] . . . manors ; in Brihtul, Fingtune (= *Brihtul fingtune* : *Bricklehampton*) x manors ; in Cumbrinctune (*Comberton*) x manors ; in Pedneshamme (*Pensham*) x manors ; in Eccyncgtinune (*Eckington*) xvi manors ; in Byrlingahamme (*Birlingham*) x manors ; in Deopanforda (*Defford*) x manors ; in Strengesho (*Strensham*) x ; in Bettesforda (*Besford*) x ; in Cromban (*Croome*) . . ; in Stoce (*Severnstoke*) x ; in Pyritune (*Pirton*) x ; in Wadbreorham (*Wadborough*) iv ; in Civingtune (*Chivington*) iii ; in Broctune (*Broughton*) iii ; in Piplincetune (*Peopleton*) x ; in Snoddesbyri (*Snodsbury*) x ; in Niwantune (*Naunton*) vii ; in Eadbrihtincgtune (*Abberton*) iv ; in Wihtlafestune (*near Naunton*) v ; in Flaeferth (*Flyforth*) v ; in Grattune (*Grafton*) v ; in Deormodesealdtune (*Dormston*) v ; in Husantreo (*Hussingtree*) and on Meretun (*Morton ?*) v ; in Broctune (*Broughton*) iii ; belonging to Hleobyri (*Cleobury ?*)[2] ii ; in Langantune (*Longton*) xxx ; in Poincgwic (*Powick*) vii ; in Beornothesleahe (*Barnsley ?*) iii ; in Actune (*Acton Beauchamp*) iii ; in Suthstoce (. . .?) and on Hileahe (. . .?) and on Treshaa (. . .?) and on Cyllincocotan (*Kilcot ?*)[3] and on Ealdanburi (*Oldbury on the Hill ?*)[3] and Dydimeretune (*Didmarton ?*)[3] and Badimyncgtune (*Badminton ?*)[3] and Uptun (*Upton*) xl ; in Deorham (*Dyrham ?*)[3] x ; in Longahege (*Longney ?*)[3] v ; on Lidanege (*Lidney ?*)[3] vi ; in Wiggangeate (. . .?) vi ; in Beoleahe (*Beoley*) v ; in Gyrdeleahe (*Yardley, near Birmingham*) v ; in Sture (*Stourbridge*) x ; in Bradanwege (*Broadway*) xx ; in Coltune (. . .?) v ; in Wicwennan (*Wickhamford ?*) x ; and for the purpose of making salt in two places, room for xviii pans, x at Midlewic (*near Droitwich ?*) and viii at Neodemestanwic (*near Droitwich ?*) and the site of two furnaces[4] at Wictune (*Witton, near Droitwich ?*) and a [*salt*] pan that is called Westrincge (. . .?) with a manor and a half in a place called Hortun (*Hampton Lovett ?*) shall belong perpetually to the same liberty. For at the time at which estates which were granted with devout mind to the Lord were unjustly taken away from God's Holy Church certain traitors usurping them published new hereditary Charters[5] for themselves. But in the name of the Father, Son and Holy Ghost we ordain that none of the Catholics receive the same [*Charters*], but, repudiated by all the faithful, they be accounted cursed, the ancient privilege having uninterrupted force.

And if in truth anyone become so diseased and led away by the madness of love of money — a thing we by no means desire—that he shall attempt in rash daring to infringe upon this the bounty of our munificence, let him be put out from the community of God's Holy Church, and from participation in the sacred Body and Blood of the Lord Christ, the Son of God, thro' Whom the whole world has been liberated from the ancient foe of the human race ; and with Judas the betrayer of Christ . . . . let him be reckoned ; unless first he shall have humbly

---

1 The names throughout in italics are of places that have been identified, and in Worcestershire unless stated otherwise.
2 Shropshire.　　3 Gloucestershire.　　4 Or 'refineries.'
5 This was not an infrequent occurrence ; it is said even the monks themselves sometimes adjusted their Charters and occasionally fabricated new ones on the lines of the originals, when they were careful to make the privileges as full as possible.

repented with meet satisfaction of that which he dared to do as a rebel against God's Holy Church ; nor let that apostate obtain either any forgiveness in this present life or any rest in that for which we look, but let him be thrust down into the eternal fires of the pit, and with Ananias and Sapphira be for ever most miserably tormented."

Here follows a Terrier in Saxon, and written in a different hand, and giving the boundary lines of the various estates cited, in the course of which mention is made of a very large number of place-names that have not yet been identified.[1] Latin is then resumed, apparently by the original scribe, and the document concludes with the following date and confirmation : —

"In the year of the incarnation of the Lord DCCCC · LXXII. was written the deed of this munificent gift, these witnesses agreeing thereto whose names are written crosswise below the order of precedence of each one according to the will of the Lord.

✠ I, Eadgar, King of the Angles of Britain, have confirmed this admirable gift with the sign of the holy cross.

✠ I, Dunstan, Archbishop of the Church of Canterbury, have confirmed the benevolence of this King.

✠ I, Oswald, Primate of York Minster, have given assent to this royal gift.

✠ I, Athelwold, President of the House of Winchester, have affixed my canonical subscription with my own hand.

✠ I, Ælfstan, Chief Priest of the See of London, have gladly impressed the sign of the holy cross.

✠ I, Alfwold, Overseer of the See of Sherborne, have heartily [*confirmed*] this [*gift*].

✠ I, Brihtelm, Servant of the people of God, most gladly have applauded the liberality of this King.

✠ I, Æfwold, Investigator of the Law (= *Archdeacon ?*) have impressed the mark of the holy cross at the command of the King.

✠ . . . . . . have joyfully added [*the sign*] of the holy cross.

✠ I, Eadelm, Superintendent of Commissaries, have with joy confirmed this gift.

✠ I, Kysinge, by permission of the grace of God, Shepherd of the spiritual sheepfold, have corroborated this bounty.

✠ I, Ælfthryth,[2] Consort of the aforesaid King, have subscribed this document with the seal of the sacred cross.

✠ I, Athulf, by the assistance of the Lord of the World, have confirmed this gift with the victorious sign of the sacred cross.

✠ I, Ælfric, Abbot, have subscribed.

after follow the names of :—

Æscwig, Osgar, Æthelgar, Cineweard, Foldbriht, Ælfæh, Sideman, ..., Brihteah, Godwine, Brihtnoth, and Germanus, *Abbots* ;

and :-

Ælfere,[3] Oslac, Æthelwine and Brihtnoth, *Dukes* ;

and :—

Æthelweard (*and two others of the same name*), Wulfstan (*one other*), Ælfweard (*one other*), Æfsige, Æthelsige, Wulfric (*one other*), Ælfwine, Wulfgeat, Æthelmaer, Eanulf,

---

1 I hope at some future occasion to be able to give a reprint of this portion of the Charter with the identification of some of the place-names, and also further translations, etc., of other MSS. relating to Pershore Abbey.

2 Ælfthryth was Edgar's second wife.

3 Was this the Ælfere who so shortly afterwards devasted the Monastery?

Eadwine, Ælfric (*three others*), Athelwold, Alfwold, Wulfmær, Ælfelm, Leofwine, Leofric, Ælfelm, Leofsige, Godwine, Ealdred, Ælfeah, Leofstan, Brihtric, Leofa, and Brihtric, *Thanes.*

To the aforesaid (*grants?*) there are also added the quantity of three acres and two farms in the famous city which is called by the dwellers there Worcester, which in the name of our Lord Jesus Christ I ordain to be held under the condition of the same liberty perpetually."

☧

II.

OF THE POSSESSIONS OF THE MONASTERY GIVEN IN THE WORCESTERSHIRE DOMESDAY THE FOLLOWING IS A REDUCED FAC-SIMILIE OF THE MANUSCRIPT, AND A FREE TRANSLATION.

Fac-simile of the Domesday Book, Worcestershire, relating to Pershore Monastery.

Translation:—

"THE LAND OF SAINT MARY OF PERSORE.

THE CHURCH OF ST. MARY OF PERSORE held and still holds the manor of Persore itself. There are xxvi hides[1] paying geld. There are adjacent three berewicks.[2] Civintune (. . .?), Edbritone (*Abberton*),[3] Wadberge (*Wadborough*), Broctune (*Broughton*), Edbretintune (. . .?), Wicha (*Wick*), and Cumbritone (*Comberton*). Of these aforesaid xxvi hides the Church itself now holds xxi.

5. In the demesne are v ploughs and xxiiii villeins[4] and viii bordars[5] with xxii ploughs. There are vii serfs,[6] a mill of iiis., and another mill of xs. at Pidele (*Piddle*) and xx sticks of eels. There are lx acres of meadow, a wood i mile[7] long and half-a-mile wide. In Wich a salt works rendering xxx mitts[8] of salt. T.R.E. [9]valued at xiii *li*, now worth xii *li*.

10. Of this land Urso[10] holds i hide and a half, and has there ii ploughs and ii villeins and iii bordars with i plough. There are iiii serfs and a mill of xs. It is worth ls. This land[11] Azor held and served the Church and in recognition he gave one annual entertainment to the monks or xxs, and on this agreement that after his and his wife's death the land should

15. revert to the Church. He was living on the day of the death of King Edward and holding the land, but some time after, his wife being already dead, he was made an outlaw. The said Urso holds i hide of the same land at Broctune (*Broughton Hacket*) and says that William the King gave it to him, for which he owes service to the Church. It was and is worth xs. Of this same land Robert le Despenser holds iii hides and a half at Wadberge

20. (*Wadborough*), and has there ii ploughs, ix bordars, iiii serfs and a park. It is worth xls. This land belonged to the villein's demesne, as also half a hide held by a vassal of the Abbot. Also in Wadberge is one hide of land in which were the monks' cows.[12] This was bought by Godric, a Thane of King Edward's, for the term of three lives, and he gave one annual

25. entertainment to the monks in recognition. Urso, the third heir, now holds this land, after the death of whom it reverts to the Church of S. MARY. This same Church holds BEOLEGE (*Beoley*) with a member GERLEI (*Yardley*). There are xxi hides between open and woodland. In the demesne is i plough and viii villeins, x bordars, and a Radman[13] with ix ploughs. There is a wood vi miles long and iii wide, it

30. renders xld. It was worth viii*li*, and is now valued at cs. This same Church holds STURE (*Stourbridge*). There are xx hide and in demesne iiii ploughs and xxiiii villeins, viii bordars with xi ploughs; there are v serfs and ii mills of xviis. and vid.; there is a Knight holding ii hides and ii Radman; there are xx acres of meadow. It was worth xii *li*, now worth ix *li*. This land pays geld.

---

1 A hide (fr. *hydan* = to cover) = a measure of land said by some to be so much as 120 acres, and by others varying quantities down to 60 acres; many of the Domesday names, measures, and distinctions are yet very indefinite and undecided.
2 A berewick was a part of an estate or manor at a distance, a village probably.
3 Modern names in italics.
4 A villein or villain was a servant attached to a manor or land.
5 A bordar (Lat. *bordarius* = a cottager) some say, one holding his hut or cottage at the will of the lord; the exact status is very indefinite.
6 A serf was a slave of the lowest order.
7 The word '*leuua*,' rendered mile, is uncertain, it probably was about a mile; some say 1½ and some 2 miles.
8 A *mitta* was a measure of salt = about 10 bushels.
9 T.R.E. = Tempore regis Edwardi.
10 Urso D'Abitot, Sheriff of the County, appears to have claimed and seized these and other lands.
11 At Wyre.
12 Or *in which was the Monks' dairy*, or cowhouse. *Vaccaria* = a dairy or cowhouse.
13 A Radman, some have considered such to be a freeman doing certain services more distant afield.

35. This same Church holds BRADEWEIA (*Broadway*). There are xxx hides paying geld. In demesne are iii ploughs and a priest and xlvi villeins with xxii ploughs; there are viii serfs. Total T.R.E. was worth xii*li* xs., it is now worth xiv*li* xs.

Of this same land a freeman held in T.R.E. ii hides and a half which he bought of Abbot Edmund ; this land was in the demesne. There are now ii ploughs in the demesne of the
40. Abbot for his food supply. It was and is worth xxx*s*. This land Urso claims as the gift of the King, and says he exchanged it for a manor which was in the demesne.

This same Church holds at LEGE (*Leigh*) iii hides paying geld. Of these the Abbot holds one hide in the demesne, and has there ii ploughs and xii villeins, and xxxii bordars with
45. xxix ploughs. There are ii serfs and ii mills of xs. and ix*d*., and xxx acres of meadow. A wood iii miles long and ii miles wide. T.R.E. it was worth xx*li*, it is now worth xvii*li*. Of this land one a half hides were held by ii Radmen.

It is now held by Sheriff Urso, and there are ii ploughs, ii villeins, xi bordars, and a
50. foreigner, between them all having iiii ploughs ; there are two serfs and a mill of iiii*s*. It is worth l*s*.

Of this land a third of a hide at Bradnesforde (*Brandsford*) is held by the said Urso, and there is there in the demesne i plough and ix bordars with iiii ploughs, and a mill of xx*s*. It is worth iiii*li*. Of this same hide the county says in T.R.E it belonged to the Church of
55. Pershore, and yet it was held by the Abbot of Evesham on the day of the death of King Edward, but how this was so is not known now.

In DODDINTREU (*Doddingtree*) HUNDRED[1]

This same Church holds MATMA (*Mathon*). There are v hides, but only iii pay geld. One of these v hides lies in Herefordshire in RADELAU HUNDRED (. . .?) ; this is held by
60. ii Radmen ; the county of Worcester claimed it for the use of S. MARY of Pershore, and it belongs to the aforesaid manor. In this said manor are ii ploughs in the demesne and vi villeins, xx bordars and i smith with xii ploughs. There is a mill of xxx*d*. It was worth ix*li*, is now worth c*s*. Of this manor Urso holds iii virgates[2] and has i plough, and a priest, a villein and iii bordars, and a Reve having between them iii ploughs. It is worth
65. xx*s*. Of this land Walter Ponther holds one virgate, but it is all waste. It is worth v*s*.

The County says that the Church of Pershore ought to have circet from all the three hundred hides, that is, one seam[3] of corn from each hide on the day of the feast of S. Martin where a freeman remains, and if it have more hides than these they are free.
70.   And if payment be not made on that day any who shall withhold the corn shall, after paying what he owes, be mulcted in eleven times its value, and that the Abbot of Pershore has such forfeiture from his c hides, as he would have from his own land. Of the other cc hides the same Abbot has the sum and full payment and the Abbot of Westminster has the forfeiture, as it is his land. The Abbot of Evesham has likewise of his land and all the
75. rest also."

The Gloucestershire portion of Domesday records the holding of Pershore in that County, and the following is a translation of the portion referring to it :—

"THE LAND OF S. MARY OF PERSHORE.

In RESPIGATE HUNDRED.

The Church of S. Mary of Pershore hold KVLEGE (*Cowley*). There are v hides taxed. In the demesne are ii ploughs and xiiii villeins and one bordar with vii ploughs. There are v

---

1 Some think = the area of a hundred hides, others a district having 100 men, or 100 families, and others again 100 villages.
2 A *virgate* : varies, some give 8 to the hide, others 4 = therefore from 15 to 60 acres.
3 *Summa* = a seam or load of corn, as first-fruits of harvest.

serfs and a mill of 1*d*., and vi acres of meadow, and a wood three-quarters of a mile long and one wide. It is worth c*s*.

IN GRIMBOLDESTOV HUNDRED.

The same Church holds HAVOCHESBERIE (*Hawkesbury*). There are xvii hides in the demesne v ploughs and xviii villeins, and xxv bordars with xv ploughs. There are ii serfs and vii coliberts[1] . There are iii mills of xix*s* and ii*d* and x acres of meadow. A wood of ii miles long and i wide. It was worth xvi*li*., now x*li*."

III.

EXTRACTS FROM THE VALOR ECCLESIASTICUS[2] OF HENRY VIII. CONCERNING PERSHORE MONASTERY.

" *The Temporalities of the Monastery of Pershore* were derived from the :—

Manor of Pershore.

	£	s.	d.	£	s.	d.
Rents of Assize	2	12	10			
In farm, one Close called the Orchard		6	8			
Rents of tenures at the will of the Superior	25	19	0			
Other sources	1	0	0			
Dues of the Fair		10	0			
In toto ...	30	8	6			

After deducting the salaries of John Sheldon, John Knollys, and Christopher Wadde, bailiffs and collectors, to the amount of £2 3s. 4d., and an annuity of £2 18s. 2d. to the Abbot of Westminster, it remains in the clear ... . | 25 | 7 | 0

County of Worcester—

	£	s.	d.
Manor of Mathon. W. Horton, bailiff and collector (Richard Nashe here paid £1 6s. 8d. for a tenement called the "Shepynground ") ...	26	13	4½
Tenements in the City of Worcester. Davythe Serche, b. & c. ..	3	6	0
Manor of Bradwey (*Broadway*) 53s. 4d. to J. Crasewell and Wm. Hoggys, b. & c.	135	6	9½
,, of Aylesborrowe (*Allesborough*) 20s. to W. Reve, b. & c. ...	90	4	11
,, of Abburton (*Abberton*)	18	10	2
,, of Lye. 40s. to W. Collys, b. & c.	64	17	4½
,, of Alderm'ston (*Aldermaston*)	33	18	3½

County of Gloucester—

	£	s.	d.
Manor of Cowley. J. Bruggys, seneschal, and W. Blowmere, b. & c. who receive salaries of £1 6s. 8d. and 13s. 4d.	16	19	8
,, of Langney (*Longley*)	2	0	0 *

---

1 A *Colibert* appears to have been a sort of middle tenant, between servile and free ; he held his land by service tenure.

2 In order that tranference might be made by Act of Parliament from the Pope to Henry VIII. (Act in 1534), this document was prepared, but the values were seldom fairly or fully given, and entries in very erratic order, and inaccurate are to be found. This document also contained a detailed list of the various sources of the income of Pershore Deanery, which amounted to a total of £259 11s. 3d., and from which payments up to £12 9s. 5½d. being allowed, left a balance as "clear receipts" of £247 1s. 9½d.

* The amounts are not carried forward, they are not so in the *Valor*.

Manor of Hawkysbury, glebe, &c., after paying to J. Bruggis, head
    seneschal, 53s. 4d., to Danyelis Courtt, sub-seneschal, 13s. 4d.,
    to J. Came and Artuary Lupyat, b. & c., £3 13s. 4d. 110 10 10

Total temporalities of Pershore Monastery   ...   .   **£527 14 5"**

"*The Spiritualities of Pershore Monastery* :—

	£ s. d.	£ s. d.
Chokenhyll, part of		14 14 4
Church of St. Peter at Worcester, after deducting £4 15s. 4d. ...		5 4 8
,, Abburton (*Abberton*)		2 13 4
,, Alderm'ston		10 0 0
,, Flyforde		2 16 8
,, Wadbarowe (*Wadborough*)		10 0
,, Broadway, after deducting £4		21 16 8
,, St. Andrew, Pershore—		

	£ s. d.	
Tithes of grain and hay in Wick ..	4 2 0	
,, ,, Bryklampton . ..	8 0 0	
,, ,, Penysham ...	2 6 8	
,, ,, Pynvyn	4 0 0	
,, ,, Besford	2 0 0	
,, ,, Defford ...	4 0 0	
	24 8 8	
Deduct payment to the Prior of Worcester per annum ...	13 4	
		23 15 4
,, Mathon, after deducting £8 18s. 5½d.		4 1 6½
,, the Holy Cross, Pershore		

	£ s. d.	£ s. d.
Tithes of grain and hay in Naunton	1 0 0	
,, ,, Broughton and Walcot	2 0 0	
,, ,, Pipulton	1 0 0	
,, ,, Byrlyngham	2 0 0	
,, ,, Combton Magna	3 13 4	
,, ,, Ekyngton	12 13 4	
,, ,, Chevyngton	1 0 0	
,, ,, Pershore	4 0 0	
Other tithes	6 7	
Divers payments	6 8	
Oblations on the four principal festivals	16 8	
,, to St. Edburg	7	
Marriages	3 4	
Churchings	1 8	
Funerals	3 4	
Dominical days	6 3	
Other Sources	6 6 8	
Tithes of lambs 10s., calves 5s., pigs 5s., geese 5s. 6d., wool 13s. 4d., hemp 2s., linseed, etc., 8s. 8d.	2 9 6	
Deaths	4 0	
Christenings	2 0	
Tithes of hay in Penysham	18 0	
Oblations to the Holy Cross	2 0	
Fourth part of tithes of corn in Straynysm	2 6 8	
	43 8 1*	

         * Disregarding any errors.

	£	s.	d.			
From which deduct :—						
Annual payment to the Archdeacon of Worcester	7	5½				
,, ,, to Edward Gregson, Rector of Fladbury, for tithes at " Pydyllmyls "	1	10	0			
,, ,, to the Abbot of Tewkesbury ...	1	8				
,, ,, ,, Bishop of Worcester ...	3	4				
,, ,, ,, Prior of Worcester ...	3	4				
,, ,, to Henry Smythe for daily celebrations of divine service for the soul of Ade Harvyngton, in a certain chapel in the Church of St. Edburg, in Pershore	6	0	0	8	6	1*

					£	s.	d.
					35	2	3½
,, Hawkesbury, after deducting 13s. 4d.					28	4	3
Total of *Spiritualities*					£143	9	1
Total of *Temporalities*					527	14	5
					£676	3	6

From the total of receipts deduct payments as follows :—

	£	s.	d.			
Salary to Gilbert Talbot, Knight, head seneschal	4	0	0			
,, Daniel Courtt, sub-seneschal		13	4			
,, W. Horton, general receiver of the Monastery	6	13	4			
,, Thomas Pynfold, auditor to the Monastery	6	13	4			
Corrody to William Ruggeley by order of the King . .	3	0	0			
for a gown annually		16	0			
for two loads of hay annually		8	0			
for the use of the poor annually	10	15	1			

						£	s.	d.
						32	19	1
Net Annual Income of the Monastery						*£643	4	5"

IV.

THE REGISTERS, ETC., HAVING PERISHED IN A FIRE IN 1287 A.D. A COMMISSION WAS HELD TO ASCERTAIN THE ESTATES, ETC., BY EVIDENCE OF WITNESSES. THE FOLLOWING IS AN EPITOME OF THE STATEMENTS GIVEN.[1]

First Walter the Prior being examined, saith, the Monastery of Pershore had certain privileges granted them by the Pope ; that the grant was burnt in the late fire, but that there was one copy remaining ; that Malgerus, Bishop of Worcester, when he came to Pershore to ordain, went to the Chapel of S. Andrew, and being invited, came to the Monastery. He says likewise that when the said Bishop was invited by the Abbot and Convent to say mass, and celebrate the feast of St. Eadburgh, being shewn their privileges, he restored the oblations which he was preparing to carry away ; and that Gervase, Abbot of Pershore, in a synod held by W. de Bleys, claimed, and had place at the Bishop's right hand.

---

* Disregarding any errors.
1 Nash, Worc. ; the Latin text is in Dugdale Mon., vol. ii. ; the MS. in the Brit. Mus.

Being asked concerning the right of sepulture, he said, that the bodies of all those who held land in the following towns were to be buried in the Abbey of Pershore, namely, all the town of Pershore, the villages of Pendefene (*Pinvin*), Besford, Defford, Wodemancote, Burlingham, Pensham, Wick, Brithlenton (*Bricklehampton?*), the whole village of Eckinton, Strensham, Wolhaesham, Nafford, Pirton, Stoke, Naunton, Great Comberton, Pipleton, North Piddle, Edbrithtun (*Abberton*), Flavel, Broughton Martin, Hussintree, Snodsbury, Upton, Coulesdone, Broughton, Walcot, Chivinton, Caldewell, Wadborough, Thorndon, Hareley, and Little Comberton; those who did not enjoy lands were to be buried in the Churchyard of Little Comberton.

He said, likewise, concerning the wills of such persons, that the principal legacy ought to be carried before the body of the deceased into the Church of Pershore, and there to be valued by the Sacrist, and the Chaplain of the place to which the deceased belonged; after the valuation made, one half to remain with the Sacrist, the other half to go to the chaplain of the place to which the party belonged; he said, likewise, it was in the option of the Sacrist to retain the whole, and pay the value of one-half to the Chaplain; all offerings offered for the dead in the monastery were to remain with the Sacrist. He said, the bodies of the deceased ought to be carried to the chapel to which they belong, and that Mass should be there said for their souls, except those of Wick, S. Andrew's in Pershore, Brickehampton, Pensham, Birlingham, and those of the fee of Walter de Nafford; that the oblations offered in the said chapels belong to the Chaplains; he said, likewise, that the Rector of the Chapel of S. Andrew had deprived the Monastery of one thrave of corn from every virgate of land in Snodesbury, Upton and Coulesdon.

Then follows the evidence of fifteen other witnesses, eight of whom were monks of this house, confirming, and adding to the above, among them was:—

Robert de Malvern, an old man, who said that the whole tithe of corn of the demesne of the Abbot of Pershore belonged to the abbot and monks; and likewise all the small tithe; he said likewise that half the corn tithe of the whole town of Pershore, except the tithe of the demesne of the Abbot of Westminster, belonged to the Abbot and Convent of Pershore; and that the half of the tithe of corn, as well of the freemen and of the villains of Wick, did of old belong to the Abbot and Convent of Pershore, and likewise of Bricklehampton, and Great Comberton, except that in Soevecurt in the said village, and in Pendesenne and in Piplintune they receive only the third sheaf; he said, likewise, that they had the third sheaf of the whole village of Eckinton, except the demesne of the Lady Constance de Lega (*or Leigh*), from whence they receive nothing, and except the tenth sheaf of seven virgates of land in the same village belonging to S. Peter's at Worcester; the third part of the tithe of flax in the said village belonged to the Abbot and Monks of Pershore; the third part of tithe corn of Strensham belonged to them, as did the half of the great tithes of Berford, Defford, and Woodmancote.

Richard Fitz Andrew, of Leigh, on his oath, said that two parts of the tithe of corn and hay of all the fee of the Abbot and Convent of Pershore at Leigh belonged of right to the said Abbot and Convent, and that the third part belonged to the Church of Leigh; the Convent of Pershore likewise received one mark from the said Church; the Convent likewise receive the first legacy from the customary tenants as due to the parson of Leigh, which Church received all the oblations.

x

Allday Ltd., Edmund St., Birmingham.

CPSIA information can be obtained at www.ICGtesting.com
Printed in the USA
BVOW01s1146010714

357895BV00004B/11/P

9 781293 193037